THE TIFFANY BOX

a memoir

Kathleen Buckstaff

TWO DOLPHIN PRODUCTIONS
SAN FRANCISCO

The events described in this book are real.
Some names of people have been changed.

Photo credits: front cover photo of Francie Mallery and Kathleen Mallery,
back cover photo, interior photo — by Richard Mallery;
cover photo of Tiffany box by the author.

The author gratefully acknowledges Regina Bidstrup, Kay Driggs,
Elizabeth Dunn, B.J. Freeman, Maria Garcia, Jeanne L. Herberger,
Mary W. Hudak, Sharon Mills, and Phil Stevenson for
their permission to reprint their cards and letters.

Acknowledgement is made to the following, in which various forms of this
book's pieces first appeared: *Los Angeles Times:* "Milk Run," "Highchair
of the Decade," "Daddy's Girl," "Post-Its and Motherhood" * *The Arizona
Republic:* "Men, Chocolate and Roses," "A Bridesmaid's Diet," "White Peach
Season," "Dance with Me," "That's My Girl," "Flight Instructions," "A Liberated
Woman," "Tricking the Tooth Fairy," "11 Months Pregnant," "Sliding Curtains."

Publisher's Cataloging-In-Publication Data
(Prepared by The Donohue Group, Inc.)

Buckstaff, Kathleen, 1966-

The tiffany box : a memoir / Kathleen Buckstaff. -- 1st ed.

p. ; cm.

ISBN: 978-0-9887642-0-0

1. Buckstaff, Kathleen, 1966- 2. Adult children of aging parents--Family
relationships. 3. Caregivers--Psychology. 4. Cancer--Patients--Family
relationships. 5. Mothers and daughters. 6. Grief. 7. Autobiography. I. Title.

HQ755.85 .B83 2013

306.874/3   2012956072

Book design by Shannon Bodie, Lightbourne, Inc.
Illustrations by Jann Armstrong

FIRST EDITION

10   9   8   7   6   5   4   3   2   1

This story is dedicated to Francie Mallery.

Contents

an e-mail

To: Lisel, Mark, Ali
From: Kathleen
Date: December 14, 2001
Subj: peace

My mother died last night. We were there, my dad, my aunt
and I. I felt like a midwife. My mom struggled. She struggled
for several hours. I put one hand behind her heart, the other
behind her back, and then she seemed to stabilize. The nurse
said my mom could stay that way for hours. I removed my
hands and stood. It was almost sunset. My dad asked me
if I were going to the kitchen would I please get him some
grapefruit juice.

I went to the kitchen, opened the fridge and poured my dad
some juice. I was anxious to go back to the bedroom — I
turned to walk down the hall and then I heard my mom say to
me in my mind, "They need to eat."

I stopped. "I don't have time," I said, telling her I wanted to get back to her.

"There's time," she said. "They need to eat."

I looked around the kitchen. There were bananas and I almost grabbed three, but then that didn't feel quite right. I opened the fridge and there was my mother's bread.

Maria, my mother's housekeeper, makes it now. It's the same bread my mom has been making for over thirty years. Whole wheat. Fresh, ground wheat. Honey whole wheat. I cut three slices, toasted them, put butter on one for my aunt and blackberry jam on the other two for my dad and me. I carried the juice and the bread and walked down the hall.

I offered a piece to my aunt, took mine and handed my dad the cup and the plate. I laughed and told them that my mother had insisted we eat. I told them the nurse and the doctor thought she'd go with more medicine, but that I wondered if we ate, if she'd relax and go.

And then Mary Lou, my aunt, and I witnessed the sunset. Gold light filled the sycamore tree that still held its leaves over my mother's room. And it felt as though the universe opened.

I could feel others there. My grandmother, my grandfather. My mother's grandparents. A childhood friend of my mother's. "Go to Mama Forest," I said to my mom. That was my grandmother. "Reach for her, she is here."

We ate the bread. Devoured it. And as I relaxed, savoring bread and jam, one hand on my mother, my dad called out, "Something is changing," and we looked. "She's leaving us," he said. "We love you so much."

And then the phone started ringing and the nurse came in and said my mom's doctor from Tucson called sending his love.

And then Dan walked in.

And I think when Dan came in the front door, it was the last oomph my mom needed. You know when you make a soup and it isn't quite right, and it needs one more key ingredient to get everything working perfectly together? Well, that is what Dan was. My mom could hand off the care of me and my dad to him. Dan stood there with his hand on my back, while my mother took her last breath and her heart stopped beating.

She needed us to eat and then she could go. No mother could die at dinnertime with her family unfed. And it wasn't until later that I realized, we broke the bread, her bread and ate it. "Do this in memory of me."

My mother died December 13, 2001 at 6:30 PM — exactly thirty-eight years from the day and hour my father asked her to marry him. It was just past sunset.

Now she is at peace, and I could feel her joyful to be alive and to not be suffering. I could feel her elated that she was alive. I could feel her love. And it was beautiful.

dear reader

I am going to imagine we're sitting down to have tea in my kitchen. I have a cupboard full of tea boxes. Let's see, I'll clear dishes off the kitchen table and put the whistle top down on the kettle. When the water boils, we'll hear it. And I'll need to know if you'd like milk or honey. While we wait, I'll tell you a story.

Last December, my friend Ali came to my house with a stack of papers in her arms. "I saved these for you," she said. "I thought you'd want to read them someday."

"What are they?" I asked.

"They're e-mails you wrote to me — from when your mom was sick," she said. "I don't know if you're ready yet, but you need to have them."

My thoughts were cast back in time — I was working as a humor columnist. I had three children under the age of eight. Dan, my husband, and I were living with my mom and dad in Arizona while we remodeled a house across the street. And then my mom was diagnosed with cancer. I was learning how to be a mother to my own children when overnight, it seemed, I had to learn how to be a mother to my own mom. The women in my mom's family live to be in their 80s and 90s. My mother's own mother had only recently passed away. My mom was 59 when she died.

I took the e-mails. When I was ready, I read them, and then I went to my garage and started looking for more. In one box, I found an old computer of mine. In another box, I found a diary. I went through many boxes, but there was one box I avoided. It was a bright blue Tiffany box, from the jewelry store on Fifth Avenue in New York.

This was the largest Tiffany box I'd ever seen. All Tiffany boxes are good — the big ones and the little ones. This one had contained a wedding present for Dan and me — a Waterford crystal vase. My mom and I agreed it was the prettiest vase we'd ever seen. The crystal catches sunlight and sends bits of color all over the walls.

I kept the empty Tiffany box on a shelf in my garage. After my mom died, I put her correspondences there. I put other things there too and with an indelible, black marker I wrote "FRANCIE" on the side. As an afterthought, I wrote, "SAVE." For years, whenever I saw the box on the shelf in my garage, I read, "SAVE FRANCIE," and the words broke my heart.

The hard part about grief is that you forget. You miss the person so much — so very, very much that the sadness is overwhelming and you forget. I forgot. I forgot what my mother had shown me — in how she lived and how she died. Any time I saw that box on the shelf in my garage, I associated it only with her death.

I finally opened the Tiffany box. Inside, I found photographs of grandchildren my mom had taped to her hospital room wall. I found letters friends had sent to her. I found copies of more e-mails I had written. I found my mother's collection of my columns. Every time I published one, my mom would buy five copies.

"You'll want these someday," she'd say and saved one for herself.

I found sympathy cards sent to me that I'd never opened. I finally read them. People's words felt soothing and kind. For years, I thought I would find death inside the Tiffany box. Instead, I found life. I don't have all of my e-mails or letters from those years, but what I realized as I read through them is that I have enough. The story was there in the Tiffany box.

This is when the kettle whistles and I stop to make us tea.

I took the e-mails and letters and shared them with a few close friends. "You have to do something with these," each woman said to me. Eventually, I decided to create a book using e-mails, letters, humor columns and diary entries. I corrected spelling and grammar, added nicknames for my children, removed personal information about my friends and changed most of my friends' names.

Most of my early e-mails were written to Lisel. Lisel is an artist and lives in New York City. Lisel has class, the real kind, not because she's snobby, but because she isn't. Years ago Lisel was my roommate. She begged me to say tomahto instead of tomato and showed me how to walk with confidence. We reconnected after I had my second baby and she had her first. We were both trying to figure out how to be mothers and artists. During the years Lisel and I wrote e-mails, it was like having a roommate again. When I was really lonely as a new mother, I wrote Lisel because it was as necessary as breathing.

Many of my later e-mails are written to my friend Ali. During this time, Ali was living in L.A. and starting a family. In college, Ali was a senior when I was a sophomore. She's the big sister I always wanted, loving, bossy and strong. Ali loves to garden. She always has something sprouting in an egg carton on a windowsill in her home. When my mom was sick, I wrote to Ali because I knew I could lean on her. I also knew that what was sacred and beautiful to me would be sacred and beautiful to her. I knew she would treat my e-mails as prayers. I did not know she would save them.

I've included e-mails I wrote to Mark. Dan and I knew we'd be friends with Mark the day we met him. In college, Mark was a freshman and we were seniors. Mark's like a kid brother, full of humor and fun. When I was taking care of my mom and three little kids, Mark reminded me that I had my own groove — "Yeah, yeah, yeah, I know the kids are sick, I know your mom is sick, that's rough, really rough stuff, but what's up with you?" Mark's originally from New York and lived in New York City when I was writing him e-mails.

And now I'd like to share with you what I found in the Tiffany box. Hold it dear. It's my story.

This might be a good time to switch from tea to chocolate. In my house, I hide dark chocolate behind the tea boxes in the cupboard on the right.

xxoo Kathleen

Part I

lavender roses

our holiday letter

December 1995

Dear Friends,

Hello! After much change, our lives have seen glimpses of routine and stability.

Dan is still running a soft-serve frozen yogurt company. He's building an exciting team of employees and is working on introducing a frozen dessert concept. As a father, he has perfected the art of fort-making. His greatest design used a hula-hoop and string to support an interior atrium. Dan turned 30.

Sunshine is 3-and-a-half and can ride her bike to her friend's house. She is filled with an eagerness to do everything: glue, paint, write, dance, cook, play pretend, sing. When asked what she wanted to be when she grew up, Sunshine replied, "A teenager."

Sweetness is one. He eats five meals a day and laughs more than he eats. He likes to climb, especially when no one is in the room. He has climbed out of strollers, grocery store carts, up ladders and onto tables. When he's not climbing, he runs, which increases the severity of his wipeouts. He just learned how to stick out his tongue and practices this trick on strangers. When Sunshine blasts music and dances, Sweetness is right there with her doing his personal rendition of the new-walker, diaper-bottomed jitterbug.

This year I started writing again. I am working on a collection of short, personal stories about pregnancy and motherhood. I have a sitter who comes to our home 12 hours a week. My life is better balanced and I have a sense of purpose and work outside of the children. I am almost sane again.

The best thing that happened to our relationship this year was that both children started going to bed at 8:00 pm. This means that for the first time in years, Dan and I have time for each other.

We wish you all the best. Our love to you,

Kathleen, Dan, Sunshine and Sweetness

To: Lisel
From: Kathleen
Date: May 23, 1996
Subj: Listen to this…

Yesterday Sunshine said to me that we needed to go to the ranch. She said it with great urgency. I told her she was going soon with my parents, but she insisted I needed to go too because in her words, "God lives near the ranch and Mama Forest is with God. God lives in the mountains and if you want to see her, there is a very big door and if you open the door you can see all the people who live with God."

This from a girl who isn't four yet.

xxoo

To: Lisel
From: Kathleen
Date: June 17, 1996
Subj: Happy Fathers' Day!

We had a great weekend at the ranch. Did I tell you Sweetness is horse-crazy? We only have one horse now and his name is Blue. Sweetness runs around screaming, "Blue, Blue, Blue," and then he goes to the fridge and gets carrots to feed Blue. Later we had a picnic in the tree house.

I'll talk with you soon.

xxoo

P.S. I have a piece on my grandmother that I wrote and I'll send it to you.

Written 1996
Published Tuesday, June 8, 1999
The Arizona Republic

Men, Chocolate and Roses

We thought my grandmother Forest was going to die many times. One time, we even thought she was dead. Three handsome paramedics arrived at her home, transferred her to a flat bed and wheeled her down the walkway. They were almost to the ambulance when Forest whispered to my mother in a soft, Georgia accent, "Get my lipstick." That's when we knew she'd live.

Another day arrived when we were certain it was her last. Forest lay in bed at home, not eating, breathing rapidly as her lungs filled with fluid. "In the freezer," she instructed. A few minutes passed, as she garnered energy. "A shoe box… Mexico… on it." Under frozen bacon and coffee beans, we found a shoebox tied shut with the word "Mexico" scrawled in her free-flowing hand. She had traveled in Mexico years ago. Perhaps this was some illegal drug, a way to make dying easier. We untied the string and removed the lid. Inside we found six bars of dark, Godiva chocolate. "It will help," she said and held open her mouth.

One day, I went to go say good-bye to Forest. She had fallen, no broken hip, but she was bruised and hadn't spoken in a week. My daughter, Sunshine, who was 2 at the time, came with me. I placed lavender roses on Forest's bedside table. Sunshine reached to grab the petals. "Don't touch," I cautioned.

And then Forest spoke. "But how will she learn to love them? You've got to touch to love. It's all right, you may touch the flowers," Forest said. With a nod from my grandmother, Sunshine touched one petal and then smelled the flower. When Sunshine smiled, Forest exclaimed, "Oh, she likes them!" Forest had something to talk about. She was alive again.

The day I knew my grandmother was truly intimate with death, I sat at her side and I could hear my mother on the phone in the kitchen talking to the caterer. "We'll be expecting 80 people," my mother said, making plans for my grandmother's memorial service.

When my mother hung up the phone, she turned to my aunt and said, "If the caterer calls back, tell him he can reach me at home in an hour."

I pictured the caterer telephoning my grandmother's house and my grandmother answering her phone. "Yes," she'd say.

"I'm calling from Continental Catering regarding the memorial service for Forest Burgess." There'd be a long pause.

"I'm still alive," she'd say. The anger would add at least another week to her life.

But the caterer didn't call back, and my grandmother died the next day. We were there, her two daughters, a nurse and I. Before her hand lost its warmth, I tucked a rose petal in her palm and closed her fingers around it. I have speculated that Forest died in front of us just so that we would believe she had died.

As I stood there, so close to the presence of life and then death, I waited for an epiphany. One moment she was there, breathing hard, sweating, calling for help. Then she was gone. It was the closest experience to being in labor that I'd witnessed: the suffering and then the peace. I could only hope she'd been born in the other direction and had come out on the side of heaven.

But I can't picture Forest in heaven. She was made for living and loving things of the earth. I can't say for certain that heaven has men, chocolate and roses. Even now, as I cut roses, I find a particularly fragrant one and I want to share it with her. I tell myself, "She's gone, she's gone." Then I hear a firm voice with a soft Georgia accent say to me, "I'm still alive!"

To: Lisel
From: Kathleen
Date: June 20, 1996
Subj: Hi

Life here looks good today. Life is amazing with a good night of sleep.

I have a babysitter coming tomorrow and I will have a full day to myself. I've found a great Mexican furniture store — and they're having a 50 percent off sale. Cheap, great stuff — old, from the '30s and I love it. I detest the new Southwestern style of furniture. I've been holding out and now I'm going to buy a desk and a chair tomorrow.

Love to you. xxoo

To: Lisel
From: Kathleen
Date: June 24, 1996
Subj: Hi

No matter what happens this week, Sweetness made it through last week without going to the doctor!!!! And he is still off antibiotics.

New furniture should arrive here on Wednesday morning. I bought a writing desk for myself. I've been looking for years. This is an old one from Mexico. I love it and it's huge. Makes me wonder who else wrote on it and what they had to say....

I've got to run. Sweetness is taking a nap, Sunshine's at school and I have some business stuff I need to do.

xxoo

To: Lisel
From: Kathleen
Date: July 8, 1996
Subj: Re: Happy 4th

It's been too long since I've written. The wedding was amazing
and the band was great. I celebrated too much — probably
because I cried at Beth's first wedding because I knew it would
end soon. Beth was beautiful, apprehensive and scared,
but thank God, courageous enough to say despite all that
happened, yes, she can love again. I felt thankful for that
because what would life be if we didn't love, if we were too
afraid, too hurt?

You know, I must tell you, that finding you again in my life, so
close to my life, so close to me — as I open up to how much I
care about you, I realize I thought I'd lost you. When you were
here visiting, it was strange because

To: Lisel
From: Kathleen
Date: July 8, 1996
Subj: more

I just hit the send button accidentally, but what I was saying is
that when you were here visiting, it was strange because so
much has happened between then and now that I felt like you
should have been here. There are stories to share, I know, of
what happened in the middle.

But I am so glad you are here now. Let me just say that.

Love to you. xxoo

Written 1996
Published Tuesday, March 10, 1998
The Arizona Republic

A Bridesmaid's Diet

In three weeks, I have to wear a dress I didn't select in front of 217 of my closest friends. Not only did I not choose the dress, I will not be the only one wearing it.

Women go to great lengths to ensure they are clad in original attire. But this night, the night I will see college and high school friends that I have not seen in years, I will be wearing the same dress as five other women, none of whom has had children. I am a bridesmaid in a wedding.

"I am so excited," the bride told me over the phone. "I found a dress that will look great on everyone."

I strapped two children in the double stroller and we went to the mall. The dress fell in a long, straight sheath when it hung on the hanger. Then I tried it on.

Six, full-length mirrors displayed hundreds of angles of me wearing the dress and the two children crawling around the floor collecting straight pins.

"Baby's milk," I told myself as I pinched various pockets of flesh. The clumps seemed less like sweet cream and more like a serious test of my self-opinion.

The saleswoman brought me the store's pair of size 11 heels. "You just need a little height," she said.

I stood up tall and held my breath. The oversized heels made me feel like a little girl playing dress-up in an outfit she never would be allowed to wear in public.

I nursed Sweetness in the dressing room and listened to Sunshine clop around the store in size 11 heels.

When I got home, I made the obligatory phone call.

"You chose this dress so that you will look beautiful in contrast to your bridesmaids," I considered saying.

The selection of bridesmaids' dresses is the ultimate revenge. Here you have your closest female friends, the ones who didn't invite you to the slumber party when you were 13 and bought you chocolate Betty Crocker frosting at the height of acne season.

I don't want to promote female competition. In eighth grade, the same women shielded you as you hid a tampon in your sleeve and then accompanied you to the bathroom. Years later, they stood crammed in a bathroom stall and discussed what he meant when he said, "I'll call you later." The same women sent flowers when he didn't, and always called later.

"It's perfect," I said.

I hung up the phone and put on the dress. Tiny straps fell over my shoulders. I identified the visible soft spots — upper arms, chin and tummy. No need to waste energy on hidden areas.

I started a spot reduction work out. I lifted hand weights and sang motivational songs with the kids. "Here an oink, there an oink, everywhere an oink-oink."

But when I attempted sit-ups, two children sat on my tummy and I gave up. Spot reduction was not working fast enough. I would have to eat less.

I have a theory about dieting. It is called The Hand Diet. Dieting is about your relationship with your hands. Everything that goes into the mouth enters via the hands. So all dieting requires is a frank and firm discussion.

"Hands, listen. I've got this wedding. It's in a few weeks. Just hold back and then you can eat as much as you want."

Now, I don't mind a control battle with my own hands. What I do mind is when others decide to help me diet. I am not one for secrets, and my biggest error was to inform my family that I was trying to lose a few pounds.

My husband started eyeing the food on my plate. "You don't really want that, do you?" he asked.

At least he didn't say, "You don't really need that, do you?"

My mother felt inspired by my efforts and decided she would go on a diet too. We were having lunch at an Italian restaurant and I dunked my bread in a bowl of olive oil and slid the bowl towards my mother.

"No, thank you," she said, "I'm dieting."

I pushed the bowl to the far end of the table. "Bad hand," I whispered.

But my efforts were futile; I could never go back. The only new clothes I owned were nursing bras, oversized T-shirts and shorts with elastic waistbands. Once I read a 2-week-old newspaper and didn't realize it. Another time, I stood in the laundry room at 3 a.m. needing to wash wet sheets, but I couldn't find the detergent. I passed six, maybe seven minutes staring straight at it. Moments like these change a person.

I heard myself speaking with authority at the wedding, "You think sleep deprivation was bad in college. Try kids." And our friends without children would moan and keep quiet about their most recent vacations.

But these people are well versed in the current rhetoric. "Children take up money, time. You lose your freedom. Your sex-life ends. You start driving an automatic."

No wonder the birth of a child is a miracle.

By adding to the complaints about children, I realized I could only further delay any of them from joining me. Instead, I devised a mother's revenge. At the wedding, I would protect the horror stories of parenthood. To counter those postcards our friends without children mailed to us from Paris, Thailand and the new restaurant down the street, I selected my own photographs to share.

I chose a picture of the children smiling and hugging a baby doll. They might as well have been seated in a field of daisies. "Here are the kids," I imagined myself saying. The next picture captured Sunshine bopping Sweetness with the doll. I saw no need to alter the first image.

Then I found a side profile of me six months pregnant, before my feet swelled and I got stretch marks on my ankles. I practiced, "Here I am, nine months pregnant." I assured myself that I felt nine months pregnant.

The final one I selected captured Sweetness laughing, wearing blue jeans and a white T-shirt — a perfect image of what most people think newborns look like until they have one. "Here's Sweetness at 1 week." (Maybe it was a few weeks — 15, 16. Those first months blur together.)

Then I purchased thick cover-up to hide the dark trenches under my eyes. I started reading movie reviews so I could talk movies. I even bought my first girdle.

When I returned to the six-mirrored dressing room for a fitting, I put on the cover-up, the girdle and then the dress. I repeated into the mirrors, "I love having children."

To: Lisel
From: Kathleen
Date: July 11, 1996
Subj: aloha!

Oh Lisel, how to make a 4-year-old's day! It's 130 degrees
out and there's nothing to do. We peak out the front door into
the glaring heat, not even willing to risk opening it, longing for
activity, something to entertain us — it's not really quite that
bad here, but almost — and then Sunshine and I see a box
and it's for her. We bring it inside, open it and the rest of the
afternoon is spent hula dancing.

Sweetness wanted a grass skirt too. We improvised and made
one for him out of purple tissue paper and tucked it into his
swimsuit. We've been singing the song "Lovely Hula Hands"
all afternoon. Thank you for the present!

The other part of my day today, yesterday and the day before
is that Sweetness decided he's potty training. He refuses to
wear diapers. He's at about 5 percent making the potty. You
know who deals with the other 95 percent? Lovely.

But life is good here. It's been almost three weeks since we've
been to the pediatrician.

Thank you for sending such a thoughtful gift.

xxoo

To: Lisel
From: Kathleen
Date: July18, 1996
Subj: happy July 18

I've been in a weird state recently. What I've figured out is that two things are going on inside. The first is that I'm slowly realizing that my grandmother died. The realization that this is what is — is getting to me. And none of this seems to help because there is nothing I can do to change the situation.

The other thing that is really hard right now is that I am deeply missing having close girlfriends here. My closest friends don't live here and it's tough. What I would give to have a playgroup with you once a week. What this means is that I need to get out more and make an effort to meet more mothers here.

Dan is under a lot of stress at work and I'm trying to be supportive. It's tough talking about work all the time. I know this is a critical, very critical period in his life and ours for that matter, but some lightness and playfulness would be great. Things seem way too serious. I imagine you've felt this way.

The potty training saga continues. Sweetness really is improving but his communication skills are lacking. Is this a male thing?

Hello to everyone.

xxoo

Written 1996
Published Tuesday, May 19, 1998
The Arizona Republic

White Peach Season

In June 1995, doctors started to pronounce my grandmother dead. But I knew there was no way a Georgia born woman would die two weeks before white peach season.

White peaches, also known as Babcocks, hit stores the second week of July. Their lower acidity makes them sweeter than other peaches. Forest Burgess would wait until the last white peach was gone and then die.

My mother and I spent the summer locating Babcocks. We found the earliest white peaches while we were on vacation in California. We packed two crates in our luggage and checked them on the plane home.

Forest held her first white peach of the season to the light and turned it.

"Where did you find it?" she said in between breaths. "Isn't it beautiful?" I could see her consider the family rule: If you have a white peach and want to eat it in the presence of others, you share. The unspoken alternative is to eat it when no one is looking.

"I'm not hungry," I shouted. Among other health problems, Forest had congestive heart failure, fluid in her lungs.

I took the peach from her and peeled away the skin, the way she always did, careful to leave the flesh smooth and intact. Forest closed her eyes and ate one slice at a time. At 89, she could still moan with delight as sweet juice dripped from her fingers and lips.

"It's sinful the way you eat a peach," my grandfather had said to her decades ago. He didn't know how to love peaches, only that white peaches commanded a premium — an extra few cents a pound. Eventually they divorced over the issue.

The women in my family can talk about a peach longer than men can talk football. The art of selecting a good peach is passed from mother to daughter. We learn early how to sniff a ripening peach, press the skin at the stem's base and listen by thumping with the flick of a finger to the quality of the core.

The women in my family also teach that as a mother cares for a child, so a daughter will care for an aging parent. For her last seven years, Forest was bedridden and my mother oversaw the details of her life. My mother waited for hours for a doctor to return her call, transferred bags of library books into and out of the trunk of her car and arranged fresh cut roses in old mayonnaise jars. She handled the weekly surprises: the broken water line, the burglary, the empty oxygen tank.

"They increased her medicine a week ago," my mother said as she sorted Forest's pills in a muffin tin. "She's lethargic now. Maybe she needs potassium. I'll call the doctor and get a blood test ordered."

I watched my mother so involved and thorough.

"What would happen to her if I weren't here?" my mother asked.

I wondered what would happen to my mother if I'm not there when she is dying.

My mother loves white peaches too. She hoards them. She shares makeup, clothes and jewelry with ease, but not peaches. During Babcock season, you're likely to find peaches in her kitchen tucked behind the toaster or in a cupboard under a salad bowl. I can't imagine her so frail that she couldn't hide a peach.

That summer, my mother and I thought we had purchased every last Babcock and that white peach season was ending. By chance, I saw some straggling Babcocks in an organic health food market stacked in a corner between Mexican peppers and persimmons. I bought the remainder and went to see Forest.

"I hear you don't have an appetite," I yelled at a woman whose body folded into the hospital bed.

She saw the peaches. "I do for Babcocks," she said.

Slowly her hand moved from under bed sheets and reached out for the peach. It seemed a long reach. For a moment, the peaches pulled her back to things of this world, as she ate one slice.

As the weather warms, I find myself looking for memories of my grandmother in the produce aisle of the grocery store. While I wait for white peaches, I realize that I was wrong to have offered Forest that last white peach. I should have eaten it in front of her, slice by slice and not shared a bite. Maybe the desire and the anger would have kept her alive until the next white peach season.

To: Lisel
From: Kathleen
Date: July 23, 1996
Subj: Re: Monday, Monday, la la la la la la

On the subject of babies — Dan and I were just discussing when to get pregnant again. I'm certain I want a third child. Dan likes life with two quite a bit and says he'd have three or four if we could skip me being pregnant and the first 18 months. What an attitude! I'm the one who suffers. But he does suffer with me. I told Dan that I had made a New Year's Resolution not to get pregnant in 1996 and Dan's response was "When has anybody ever kept a New Year's Resolution?"

The trouble is that I'm really not much fun when I'm pregnant, or at least that's been the case for the last two. I puke several times a day for months. But I'm also of the mindset of — I really want another child — why not just jump in, go for it and get through it, instead of looking at the future with impending dread?

I keep thinking there is another little boy out there for me. I'm not sure why I think that, it just feels that way, sort of dreamlike. But the question is when. I don't know yet. I'm loving the kids. Sunshine's tough, but she's always tough and she's challenging for great reasons — she has a ton of energy and loves doing things and engaging in life. But that child wears me down. I need breaks and have to keep constant friends and activities going for her. But I'm digressing — I suppose that's because I don't know when we'll get pregnant. It's a mystery to me.

Dan's on the line! I'll talk to you soon.

xxoo

Written 1998
Published Tuesday, September 15, 1998
The Arizona Republic

Dance With Me

I always assumed that when a couple got married it meant they could dance together — not rock and roll, do your own thing, but couple dancing — where the only way it works is when the man leads and the woman follows.

As a girl, I watched grown-ups dance. I could always pick the couples who had danced together for decades because they moved without hesitation. I didn't care if their day lives were fraught with conflict. To me, if they could dance together, it meant they knew true love.

Before our wedding, my husband and I took dance lessons. I even got Dan to practice with me. I think the fact that he was going to have an audience helped his motivation. On the big day, we were ready to look like a married couple on the dance floor. Dan wore a rented tux and I dressed for the fairy tale. After we said our "I do's," the band played "Love Makes the World Go Round." We had practiced to the record version many times, but the live band played it slower.

I believe Dan was keeping time to the record song in his mind. A little faster and we could have danced double time. All I could hear was the band. When I slowed to the beat of the band, Dan thought I was protesting his inexperience. I had done this in the past, but I had promised to try to follow during the wedding dance. A few more measures passed and we were in a fight for the lead. Dan ended the dance early, but I believe that was because the song in his mind finished before the band did.

Over the years, I taught Dan a few dance moves my father did. But it is a tough situation when a woman begins a sentence with, "This is how my daddy always did it…." So we stuck to rock and roll, where we could each dance to the beat the way we each interpreted it. Then I saw an article in the newspaper. It said, "Free Dance Instruction, Borders Bookstore, Saturday night." I told Dan I had a babysitter and that we were going to take lessons that night.

"There are some good movies playing," Dan said.

Together we climbed the steps to the second floor of the bookstore to the music section. It was a late summer night and the air was hot. The aisles in between the CD racks were lined with people waiting to learn to dance. Before the instruction began, I went to the bathroom. I needed to fix my hair, put on lipstick — do something. I wanted to look good. I'd just dragged my husband up two flights of stairs to take swing lessons in a bookstore because I believed he and I needed to dance seamlessly together by the time we were 60.

I'd been in that bathroom before — usually it was quiet. But that evening it buzzed like a girls' bathroom before a school dance. Girls and women stood on tiptoes to catch their reflections in the mirror. Together we primped, fixing lipstick, bra straps and nose rings.

Back in the music section, I squeezed through layers of people. I found Dan thumbing through a sports magazine.

"Football season is starting," Dan smiled. "Maybe we could catch some highlights on TV at home."

Then the instructor began, "I'm Steve. If you don't have a partner, find one." He waited a minute. "Leads start with your left. Follows start with your right."

Around me, couples took hold of each other's hands and I heard people introducing themselves. One older man wearing a plaid shirt said to his dance partner, "My daughter made me come."

Dan and I faced each other. I don't think we had ever started with the basics. Dan always approached swing dancing as if it was football and he was running a pattern. Execute the move. Music was extraneous.

Steve put on music and counted, "Slow, slow, quick-quick. Step, step, rock-step."

I watched Dan listen and struggle to find the beat. "He's changing his words," Dan said, frustrated that the instructor was alternating slows, steps and numbers. We started and stopped, started and stopped. We bumped into another couple.

"Sorry," we said. "Sorry," they laughed.

"Move us closer to that couple," I pointed to the man wearing the plaid shirt. I wanted to hear what they were saying.

"I drove all the way here from Chandler," the woman said. He spun her around and her floral skirt twirled. She laughed. He looked pleased. This was much better than a movie.

Steve walked us through another spin move and counted out the steps. One couple asked Dan to teach them the move he had just tried.

"Did you pay them?" Dan asked me.

"Five dollars," I said.

The music played, "How lucky can one guy be?" and Dan and I did one spin perfectly in time to the music where he led and I followed. I wondered how lucky could one gal be.

There was nothing textbook romantic about the night. The lights were fluorescent and bright, good for reading. The music was faint and hard to hear. The floor was institutional carpet. Nothing made for gliding or twisting. Someone set up a table and sold bottled water for $1.50. But people were dancing.

Afterwards, Dan and I walked down the stairs together. "It's been my policy only to do things that I'm naturally good at," Dan said. In other words, he was saying, I wasn't very good at this, but I tried for you.

Maybe we did discover true love on the dance floor.

To: Lisel
From: Kathleen
Date: August 14, 1996
Subj: Grrr

I'm still in Del Mar. I'm getting to know a mom next door and it's nice to have girl time. She has three kids —15, 10 and 2. I really enjoy her company but watching what she's going through with her teenager makes me shudder. Lisel, our lives are dreamy now compared to the teenage stuff.

Dan gets in late tomorrow night. He's taking off Thursday and Friday. I am such a better person when he's around. Much calmer. And I'm realizing how much I depend on him for adult conversation. My life can be a bubble with no reason to leave it.

I'm getting ready for school to start. Sunshine needs it. She's quite bored or at least has her moments. Like today, for example, when she used a bottle of toothpaste to place handprints on her bedroom wall. I suppose finger-painting is encouraged. One might even applaud her creativity. Grrr.

I decided to clean it up in the morning. Earlier today she split a cherry in half and smudged it on the wall behind the dining room table. Sweetness is still heavily in the throes of potty training. I'm ready for him to make his final passage.

Hope you are well.

xxoo

Written 1996
Published Tuesday, November 17, 1998
The Arizona Republic

That's My Girl

It's school picture time again. The notice arrived home today: "Just for one day, clean up your kid." It didn't say that, but it might as well have. I remember the year my daughter was 4. That year, I felt like the form letter from the school photographer had been addressed personally to me.

Sunshine wore the same white cotton sundress every day that year. I hoped something would convince her to change outfits. Maybe cold weather would deter her. Maybe children at school would tease her.

But each morning, she appeared from her room wearing the same dress. It was her way of beating the system. The other kids had to leave their security blankets, bears and dolls at home, but she took what was most dear to her to school every day: she wore it.

I wanted to be a big person on picture day, I really did. I wanted it not to matter to me that the other girls would be wearing clean dresses with matching bows and there would be my daughter in a tattered, stained sundress. I wanted it not to matter that the mothers at school would look at the girls, look at my daughter, and then look at me. But picture day seemed more about me than my daughter. The night before picture day, I placed a new dress on Sunshine's bedside table. It felt weak of me.

The next morning, when Sunshine danced out of her room wearing the sundress, I asked if she'd seen the new dress.

"It's picture day, mom," she said and did a twirl — as though I had forgotten. Then she draped pink plastic beads around her neck for the occasion.

"You might be cold," I said.

"I don't care," she said and patted the bangs flat across her forehead.

I deferred to an authority and read out loud the form sent home from the school photographer: "Sleeveless dresses and pale colors are not recommended."

Sunshine put her hands on her hips, held her chin up and said, "I don't care."

But I did care. Her dress of choice, the one that made her feel beautiful, brought out ugly things in me. I wanted to insist — "If you're going to wear the same dress everyday, at least wear one I like."

My mother had bought the sundress at a craft fair. The collar was never basted down and the straps were too long. But I worried if Sunshine chose her dresses for me, eventually she'd choose her husband for me. Blame can work like that on mothers. I held my words.

Then I considered appealing to her sense of compassion: "I will look like a bad mother if you wear that dress." My emotions weren't pretty or kind. I was being socially self-conscious and I knew it. I saw I was capable of caring more about the appearance of love than love itself. I held my words.

I looked at Sunshine. There she was, a 4-year-old girl standing in our kitchen, hands on her hips, chin up, draped in pink plastic beads and dressed in the sundress. In her moment of defiance, I realized that when the photographer's camera flashed, he wouldn't capture just a girl, any girl, but it would be my girl and all her spirit. That day, I let her wear the dress, and when I saw the proofs from the photographer, I recognized my child as my own.

That year, on picture day, I saw that there was as much for me to learn from my daughter as I could hope to teach her. Still, when I receive the form letter from the school photographer, I start wanting to make my children different from who they are. Then I stop and ask myself if I can remember what it was like to not care. Could I show up to school for the entire month of November wearing a sundress and pink plastic beads? If someone asked why I was wearing the same clothes, I'd most likely wring my hands, shuffle my feet and say, "I'm trying to not care so much what others think of me. What do you think? Want to try with me?"

But what I'd really like is to be able to wear the same outfit for a month. If anyone questioned me, I would stare them down, my boldness larger than my size, and I'd say with the ease and assurance of a 4-year-old girl with hands on hips and chin up, "I don't care."

To: Lisel
From: Kathleen
Date: August 27, 1996
Subj: new body

I am home!!!!! It's nice to be back with Dan. We saw each other on weekends while I was at the beach but it was hectic and fast, lots of people and little time.

My good news is that I inadvertently exercised a ton in Del Mar — stairs in the house, sand walking, pushing kids in the beach stroller and swimming everyday. I feel healthy and fit for the first time in years. Dan finds the new body quite sexy, so that's nice. Just in time to get pregnant again.... But not yet!

That's all for tonight. I was glad to hear from you.

xxoo

To: Lisel
From: Kathleen
Date: September 4, 1996
Subj: chaos

What a joy it is to know that summer is ending and life should be settling down, if in fact, life ever does settle down. I still haven't figured out preschools or babysitters or my life, for that matter, but I'm calmer about it now. A friend of mine who is living in a commune has a saying. She always says, "It will become clear."

I'm also considering getting a dog. This is a big step for me because I am not a dog person. I do not like dogs nuzzling my crotch. I also do not like dog slobber anywhere near my earlobes or ankles — or on any other body part. I can think of a gazillion reasons why I don't want a dog. But I think it would be good for our family, add some chaos and some love. Can you believe I would want to add more chaos to my home?

xxoo

To: Lisel
From: Kathleen
Date: September 14, 1996
Subj: oy vey!!!

It's almost midnight on Friday night and nothing, and I mean nothing, seems clear. Even my desk height on my new (old) desk is wrong, so I'm sitting on a pile of pillows.

I'm concerned my mom is swaying me towards choosing a Montessori preschool because it's closer to her and would give her easy access to us. My mother is notorious for giving advice based on what brings her children and grandchildren closer to home.

Fortunately, Sweetness is healthy and great. He spent a day with a woman who watches a few kids in her home and it went well, but I had Dan home from work with a fever so my workday didn't happen.

xxoo

Written 1996
Published Tuesday, April 21, 1998
The Arizona Republic

Flight Instructions

Sweetness awoke screaming at 4:12 a.m., tugging on his left ear. No reasonable amount of holding, singing or Tylenol could convince him that going back to sleep was a good option. Together, we waited for the newspaper and the pediatrician's office to open. Before it was even light outside, I was already canceling the day.

We had been at the pediatrician's office the day before with Sunshine, who had an ear infection. I did think to ask, "Since we're here, would you just peak in Sweetness's ear?" But Sweetness looked so content as he worked to fit a toy carousel into his mouth. He's fine, I told myself.

When we returned to the doctor's office, I crept back into the waiting room and tried not to think of what the nurses would say.

"Wasn't she just here yesterday?" one would say.

"She's wearing the same outfit," another would reply. "A few days must have elapsed."

No one said any of these things that I am aware of. Instead, they were sympathetic, which is what I really wanted.

The truth is that I like this pediatrician and the nurses and the receptionists quite a bit. Sometimes I wonder if I do find excuses to go there just so I can have adult interaction. Sweetness was diagnosed with an ear infection and I was not shy with the prescription sheet when we filed back into the waiting room. I let it flit about as if to announce, "This is not a symptom of my loneliness. He is sick."

The children and I spent the remainder of the day watching videos.

Anxious for bedtime, I served dinner at 4. None of us had slept well in weeks — the ear infections followed high fevers and colds. Because the children finished dinner early, it was still light outside. I put on their jackets, socks and shoes and we ventured out. The fresh air felt clean and invigorating compared with the sick air inside — or maybe it was just that we were all in the middle of our Tylenol with hours to go before it wore off.

I sat in a plastic chair and watched the children play. Sunshine made a mixture out of sand and water in a wheelbarrow. She added sand she had dyed blue at preschool to make her mixture "blue salt water." She said she was preparing a home for her pet, the sand crab she would catch at the beach next summer.

Sweetness toddled on the grass picking up leaves and rocks until he noticed the planes overhead. That evening, we were in the flight path. Every three minutes, a jet appeared small in the eastern horizon and flew towards us, growing larger and larger. The jets popped out against the gray background of an overcast sky.

Sweetness riveted his attention on each plane. As soon as he saw one on the horizon, he ran towards it, as far as the grass and wall would allow. He ran pointing. Then as the plane soared overhead, enormous compared with any toy plane he owned, Sweetness would pirouette, never losing sight of the plane, his head cast upward, body spinning. He would stretch out both arms to grab hold of it. But the plane continued on its course, and Sweetness chased it with his arms outstretched, reaching, until the plane passed out of sight behind the red-tile roofline.

I have been told that toddlers don't have an accurate understanding of distance and perspective. A plane far away is a small plane. One close is big. And grabbing for something in the sky is done in earnest, with the full intention and expectation of touching it.

The planes came again and again. With each plane, Sweetness repeated his pattern. Glued to the flight path, he pointed and ran, never looking down, never checking his step. He fell once like a row of tipped dominoes — feet trip, knees buckle, stomach flops, hands touch down. If his eyes lost sight of the plane, his mind never did. In an instant, he popped back up and kept running. He stayed focused.

That night, as I held Sweetness asleep in my arms, I wondered what my flight path was. What was it that would capture my entire attention, make me run and point, even fall and get up and keep going? The streetlight coming through the blinds cast stripes of yellow light on the wall and I could hear Sunshine breathing in the room next door. I realized that, at least for now, I held my flight instructions in my arms.

The difficult part is accepting that each morning when I awake, I never know the direction my journey will take me.

To: Lisel
From: Kathleen
Date: September 15, 1996
Subj: the next day

I'm much calmer today and I've ruled out Montessori —
it's too far away and I'm considering two other preschools.

The weather is cooling here and we've had some rain from
a hurricane that hit south of us in Mexico. We played outside
today. What a break from the 110 degree heat.

We had so much family time today, really some good playing
and hanging out. We've also started eating more meals
together and it's magical looking eye to eye with Dan and
Sunshine and Sweetness. Definitely makes me feel blessed.

I'll talk to you soon. Lots of love.

xxoo

To: Lisel
From: Kathleen
Date: December 11, 1996
Subj: need advice

What do you think — I have a cute picture of the kids for an Xmas card but Sunshine has her eyes closed. Should I go ahead and use it? She's laughing but her eyes are shut. In all of the other pictures she's making funny faces which can be frustrating roll after roll.

Dan's finished with traveling now until after Xmas and I'm relieved to have him around more. He's really been gone a lot and I'm missing him. But I'm hoping we can get a little more time together soon.

I'm running around trying to figure out how to make Christmas magical. The kids are both at ages where I think Christmas has the most magic. I should buy candles and beautiful music to fill the home with mystery and depth. That will be what the kids remember, that and all the toys.

xxoo

our holiday letter
December 1996

Dear Friends,

As 1996 comes to a close, I'm struggling to remember what happened this year. This year we thought about getting a dog. We even went so far as to purchase a large dog crate, bowls, food, toys and a cedar-scented pillow. We lived with the crate in our family room for several months. Sunshine discovered an effective way to deal with the Sweetness problem was to convince him to pretend he was a dog. In this way, Sweetness willingly crawled into the cage barking and licking the bars. By the time he had curled up on the cedar-scented pillow and was nibbling on dog biscuits, his exit door was locked. When this scenario kept repeating itself, we decided to wait to get a dog.

These days Sunshine, age 4, loves to dance and sing, but insists on an audience. If I glance at Sweetness during one of her performances, she starts again. Recently, she spent the night at her friend's house. She packed her own bag, opened the front door herself and was gone. Dan, Sweetness and I all found our house to be miserably quiet without her. When I called to check in, she told me not to worry and that she'd be back sometime next week.

Sweetness has a passion for horses, trains and any toy Sunshine is playing with. He just turned two and the word he uses most frequently is "too." This means he wants to eat sitting on a booster chair too, to pee in the potty too, to sleep in a bed too, to ride a bicycle too. His greatest sadness occurs when Sunshine goes to school and he can't go too. Sweetness's joy is that he likes to laugh and finds most things funny, except the dog crate.

This year, I decided to try to get fashionable. I had my hair highlighted, sported purple fingernail polish and bought clunky shoes. This was part of an "I may be a mom, but I don't have to look like one" phase. Although a look of sophisticated maturity was my goal, I've realized that with my chipped nails, grown-out highlights and clunky shoes, I look more like our babysitters. The best thing about my year is that I've been writing. I'm working on a non-fiction book about pregnancy and motherhood. Dan says I can write anything I want about him as long as I get paid. Right now I'm working on finding someone to pay me.

Dan's had a good year building his team at work and he's developing a wide vocabulary for describing blankets on hotel beds. This year he was detained by every major snowstorm to hit this continent. Who says you don't see snow when you live in Arizona?

In our letter last year we included one e-mail address for the two of us. Well, this has had its repercussions. I don't like Dan reading my mail, but he insists it's addressed to both of us. After some lengthy discussions, we each have our own e-mails. Despite the separation in cyberspace, we are both still living at the same address.

Please visit. We have a large, empty dog crate and an unused cedar-scented pillow. Sweetness can show you how to unlock the door. Our love to you,

Kathleen, Dan, Sunshine and Sweetness

To: Lisel
From: Kathleen
Date: January 13, 1997
Subj: big news!!!

I've had great news. It came Friday night. I had spoken to an editor from the LA Times on Thursday and then she called as I was arriving home with bags of groceries in my arms and Sweetness screaming. She told me they want to publish a series of my pieces. They are going to pay me AND she doesn't want to edit them down!!! She, like you, thinks I say what's important in the amount of space necessary. Yahoooooooo!!!!!!!!!!!!

The only concern now is the contract. I'll let you know. I'm quite excited.

I understand where you're coming from about the artist myth. But I want to let you know that no artist, totally submerged in his or her work can reflect back on society. I believe that true art requires the artist to maintain a tension between living and art. In this way Lisel, the art is informed by life and can then reflect back and inform. It is a tension filled with conflict and pressure, needs met and unmet, but in that, there is energy and energy is life. Do not stop believing.

xxoo

To: Lisel
From: Kathleen
Date: January 14, 1997
Subj: Tuesday

It's Tuesday and I'm home waiting for the closet woman to come and show me how we are going to transform half of my closet into my spiritual sanity — a place where I can write. Miracles do happen.

I miss you today. I could use hanging out in your home and making soup. Doesn't that sound nice? It's cold here and rainy. The kids love it. I don't mind it either, but it does alter the mood.

xxoo

Written 1997
Published Tuesday, April 7, 1998
The Arizona Republic

A Liberated Woman

Lately, I've realized that the only way I can be a liberated woman is if my mother is willing to make certain it happens.

As a child of the '60s and a woman of the '90s, I believe it is my birthright to live the life of a modern woman. Wasn't it my destiny to be able to have it all? Wasn't that what the picketing and protests were about? Equal opportunity. Right to vote. Right to work.

But I'm still struggling for other basic rights. The right to read a magazine article from start to finish. The right to eat a meal sitting down. The right to go to the bathroom alone. I feel these goals are attainable, I really do, but only if I have the help of my mother.

What I don't understand is why, when I became a mother, I lost my privilege as a child of my mother's. I know I had a 10-year span where I was ungrateful. It started when I was 12. Still, she continued to make my meals, take me to the doctor, pay for my clothes, help me with my homework. As each day of my life passes, I marvel at my mother, and I wonder if I apologized with great sincerity for my lack of appreciation of her, would she, could she, consider resuming some of her old activities?

I miss her taking responsibility for my life. If my mother wanted to bring over dinner every night, I wouldn't complain about the food selection. I'd even do the dishes without being asked twice. And I'm certain more time with my mother would prove beneficial to my children.

I don't seem to have the same authority my mother had with us. My mother not only potty-trained each of us before we were 2, she had all four children eating green vegetables and liver.

Why if my mother were willing to take my children four or five days a week, then I wouldn't be the woman I am. I'm one of those women who will be 50 and still wearing the same styles that were current the day I graduated from college. I'll be a tribute to a past era, a wax museum display of the '80s, except I'll be gray.

I spotted my first gray hair after six months of a colicky baby. I was living in California at the time and my mother was in Arizona, too far away to help. I figured I could either start dyeing my hair or move back to Arizona. We moved back home.

The move back home was a bet that my mother wouldn't let me rot. She'd stand to lose a lot if I did. With all that time she invested in me, it was my conviction that she wouldn't be able to tolerate the regression I've experience since having children. She would have to prop me up, provide ground support. Could she really stand to see my white laundry pink? My sauces runny? My windows marked with handprints?

Much to my surprise, the answer consistently has been yes. It's the routines that are killing me. Everyday I drive to preschool and pass through four stop signs and five traffic lights. I count them. They say routine is good for children.

It provides them with a sense of security and stability. Their world is predictable. But when I'm feeling over-the-edge, I drive an extra block past school so that I can pass through a fifth stop sign, and I feel wildly rebellious when I make the U-turn and count six.

It's difficult to have been liberated and then have children. I wonder if it would have been better to have blissfully entered motherhood as a self-sacrificing angel, and then about the time the kids hit junior high, to suddenly realize my potential and individual interests.

Self-exploration and actualization before children seem like a test in delayed gratification. You spend your adolescence and early adult life figuring out who you are and what you're bad at and good at, and how to make a go of it. Then you start just as you have children and everything changes. I'm not saying the changes are for the worse or the better, just that everything changes.

Suddenly, you want your children to have everything you've had and everything you've had requires someone to do a lot of driving and that someone now turns out to be you. It's worth it, you say. But what I want to know is — how can I truly be a liberated woman if I don't have someone taking care of me?

My mother dreamed that I would attend college. I always believed that dream was for me. But as my days pass counting stop signs, I wonder if my attending college was more for her than for me.

If my mother entered me into the state fair, she'd get a blue ribbon. I thought the blue ribbon meant I was free to be me, free to do whatever it is that I wanted to do. But the blue ribbon was for my mother. It meant that now she was free to be her, free to do whatever it is that she wants to do. It showed she'd made it through preschool admissions, grade-school teachers, high school parties, and college tuition bills. She'd probably earn bonus points because, in addition to leaving the house and getting married, I've proven to be a reliable breeder.

Of course, my mother has earned this freedom. She did her time. I couldn't deny her that. It just never occurred to me that liberation of women included my mother.

I see my mother quite a bit. She swishes into my home, uses my phone to check her messages, returns a few phone calls, marvels at the children, and then tells me tidbits from the latest article she's read while I nibble on the children's toast crust.

I interrupt her, and ask her to listen to the children's coughs. I'm trying to determine whether it's the croup cough, the bark cough or the post-nasal-drip cough. My mother knows these things. She listens, answers that it's the bark cough, and suggests I call the doctor. Then she's off to a work meeting and then a social luncheon.

My mother wears palazzo pants, a black T-shirt and clunky shoes. Her hair sheens with the hues of dark coffee. She's confident. I see it in her stride. There's nothing gran-nyesque about her. She's upright, beautiful as she lives her own life. My mother is a liberated woman.

When we're out together, people stop us on the street and ask if we're sisters. My mother laughs and coos, "Oh, you've made my day!"

I run my fingers through my graying hair and wonder what happened to my day.

To: Lisel
From: Kathleen
Date: February 1, 1997
Subj: I miss you

Yesterday, I went and looked at a school a parenting teacher had mentioned. It's located in an annex off of a church. It was magic Lisel, truly magic. There are two great trees on this campus and they take children under the canopy of these desert trees and read to them there. Adjacent to it is a co-op preschool that can take Sweetness. I would love to be part of a community like this. Much more my pace than the BMW set. And the children at the school were intent and present.

I'm going with it, moving with the spirit, feeling led, certain that a path will make itself clear.

xxoo

To: Lisel
From: Kathleen
Date: February 3, 1997
Subj: read all about it!!!!!

One of my closest girlfriends called me from LA this morning crying and screaming and laughing, "You're here, in the paper, it's huge!!!" "What?" I replied. And she said it all again. But I didn't believe her because I had no idea a story was coming out so soon. Lisel, I'll send you a copy — but if you can, go and buy a LA Times Sunday paper and look at the Life and Style section. Unbelievable layout, it's the whole font page, a color picture and everything. You'll be amazed. I just started crying when I saw it. These women editors at the Times, now these are women who know how to walk boldly.

xxoo

Written 1995
Published Sunday, February 2, 1997
The Los Angeles Times

Milk Run

We were out of milk. There are certain items I need to have in my home that help me feel like I am being a good mother. When I'm out of milk, I envision the pediatrician plotting the growth charts of my children and pointing to a dip in the curve.

"Are they drinking milk?" she asks.

And I have to confess that it was not possible for them to drink milk because I didn't have any.

So we went to the grocery store.

Going to the grocery store with two children was still a new and brave experience for me. Sweetness was only 4 weeks old and Sunshine was 2. To help ensure a successful outing, I packed a bag of pretzels to occupy Sunshine while I shopped, and I nursed Sweetness immediately before we left.

Whoever invented the notion that new babies could and should eat only every four hours never met either of my children. Sunshine ate all her pretzels in the car on the way to the store, and when we pulled into the parking lot, she was thirsty.

I kept Sweetness in his car seat and attached his seat to the top of the grocery cart. Sunshine sat in the flip-down seat, and I wheeled them to the drinking fountain.

A mother pushing a cart walked by us followed by a child pushing a child-sized grocery cart. I stood between Sunshine's line of sight and the child pushing the miniature cart until they passed. Mutiny was not on my grocery list.

Sweetness was beginning to cry. Between getting two children into the car, driving, parking, loading them into the cart, locating the drinking fountain — I looked at my watch — 45 minutes had passed. He was probably hungry.

Sweetness still had his newborn cry. I am convinced a newborn's wail was designed by nature to aid in survival by triggering an instant sense of alarm and sympathy in any listener. This genetic disposition is useful, I am sure, but I found that as Sweetness yelled louder and louder, the grocery store came to a complete stop. And there I was wheeling down aisles grabbing items as fast as I could.

Sunshine, sensing my stress, climbed on her knees, turned backwards and tried sticking a pacifier in Sweetness's mouth. When he kept refusing, she yielded, reseated herself, put the pacifier in her own mouth and began sucking.

"For babies," I said.

I held the pacifier by the handle between my teeth, searched for a clean place to tuck it and tried to keep moving. We proceeded: a howling baby, a toddler repeating, "Please pacifier, I said, 'please!'" and a mother with a pacifier in her mouth.

I had been working on teaching Sunshine colors. So when we entered the produce department, we found a welcomed distraction.

"Radish! Radish!" she pointed.

"Radishes are red," I had said many times to her as I listed objects that are red.

Sunshine wanted one.

Eager to replace a pacifier fixation with a radish, I pulled one off the bunch, rubbed it on my shirt and gave it to her. Delighted, Sunshine popped the radish in her mouth. As I was bagging lettuce and tomatoes and Sweetness was still screaming, Sunshine entered her own world. She rolled the radish around her mouth, spit it out and then popped it back in again. At least she was at peace.

The cashier heard us coming and paged for help. An older woman in line let me go in front of her. I unloaded food, hand over hand, while the older woman cooed and made bird noises at Sweetness.

"This always works to calm my grandchildren," she said with confidence.

Sweetness cried harder.

Sunshine put her radish on the belt to send it through to the cashier "to pay for it."

At last, I was able to take Sweetness out of his car seat. I took a deep breath. We were making it. He was drenched and his face was almost purple. His crying slowed to a sputter, an indignant whimper.

The grocery store started to move again and everyone else seemed to take a deep breath too.

They were thinking, "She's almost gone."

As I attempted to fill out the check, one-handed, I had a difficult time keeping Sweetness's head from flopping over. When his head would drop down, he was inches from my breast and he started trying to nurse.

My milk started to come in and I felt my bra soak. I tried to crouch forward so that I wouldn't spot my T-shirt, navy blue, but was too late. I now had two wet spots, the size of silver dollars, glistening on my chest.

I planned to push Sunshine in the cart with one hand and hold Sweetness and his head over the milk spots with the other hand. But when the man bagging groceries offered to help me out to the car, I conceded that I had left my pride somewhere on aisle three and that I would not be shy about accepting his assistance.

Sunshine, who was intently watching the man bag groceries, saw we were about to leave and became frantic.

"Radish? Where's my radish?"

I looked at the man who had bagged the groceries.

He shook his head.

And then Sunshine and I looked at the cashier. She was pretty, had curly brown hair and she was blushing and chewing. Her store pin read, "Let me help make your day."

She had eaten the radish.

Sunshine started to cry. I decide to try to make this educational and started explaining to Sunshine the words "embarrass" and "blush."

"Radishes are red and when people blush, they turn red."

"I thought it just fell out," the cashier managed, still chewing the whole radish. "I like radishes," she said.

"My radish," Sunshine said.

The cashier picked up the speaker, "Produce, bring one radish to the register."

A man wearing a green apron approached us carrying one radish.

"That's for me," Sunshine said looking at the cashier.

Sunshine stopped crying and took the radish.

The cashier apologized, and then we caravanned out to our car.

And this is how I arrived home with no milk.

To: Lisel
From: Kathleen
Date: February 4, 1997
Subj: six cups of coffee

I'm a wreck and I need to find peace within myself. I don't know what I was thinking, but I don't think I ever really thought about people I don't know reading my stuff. Oh, I know that's supposed to be the goal, but I really write because it keeps me sane and I enjoy doing it and it helps me make sense of life or at least have time to explore the senselessness of it — anyway, I feel like I've had six cups of coffee and I haven't had any. I'm excited and nervous and terrified and worried and just a wreck.

I don't know what I was thinking sending my stories out into the world. I like to pull aside a select person, a true supporter and hand them a copy of a chapter or two and let them read it — and then while they do, my stomach churns and I wait. But this mass distribution, now this is mind-boggling, truly something I hadn't spent any time contemplating. I saw it as such a long-shot. I think I have some growing to do in this area. I need to let go of my pieces and let them go where they will. I'm not there yet.

xxoo

To: Lisel
From: Kathleen
Date: February 17, 1997
Subj: happy presidents' day!

I wish you were here today to hang out, chat and get me laughing. I've had a long day. But before I get into that, or maybe I'll just skip it because who needs to live a long day twice? Anyway, about the pregnancy stuff — God, do I know about worrying. Maybe you are, maybe you're not. I've found that worrying delays my period.

I feel anxious about getting pregnant. Lisel, I so want another child. The room is ready, my office is ready, but my body isn't quite yet. I've been losing weight and given my history of losing weight in the first trimester — I want to be about five pounds heavier before I get pregnant. I think I've become lactose intolerant again. I've stopped eating dairy, but consuming dairy has always been my easiest and most enjoyable way of gaining weight. My mom, the nutritionist, has put me on a steak and nut and olive oil diet. I need to have some reserves going into this.

I am thinking of you, wondering if you're pregnant. What magic pregnancy is, don't you think??? How amazing to be a woman. I tell Sunshine often that girls can have babies and boys never can. I'm trying to instill in her some of the old fertility worship and a sense of the divine in the feminine.

Good night, sweet kisses.

xxoo

To: Lisel
From: Kathleen
Date: February 24, 1997
Subj: Monday

I have another piece coming out on your birthday! What fun!
But I think you'll be gone. What day do you leave? And when
do you return? Please give me dates so I won't be too sad
waiting for your return.

Yesterday was my birthday. It was a good family day. I'm
fighting a sinus infection so I took a delicious nap. We had a
houseguest who finally left. He was terribly self-centered and
although interesting, I was relieved to see him go.

But Sunshine was the best on my birthday. She spent all
day wrapping up special items for me — a pencil with a duck
on it, cut out shapes, a stuffed puppy dog — and she made
me a card with her name and my name written on it, all by
herself. It was really sweet. I started crying when Sunshine
and Sweetness were singing happy birthday to me. Who could
want a better present than your own two children singing
happy birthday to you?

xxoo

To: Lisel
From: Kathleen
Date: March 6, 1997
Subj: news

I just received my first check from the LA Times! Now I feel rich!

Not sure what I have to tell you. Today after school, Sweetness got a kick out of playing with a broken water fountain. He climbed up a stepstool, pushed the button and SQUIRT, water shot out three feet. He'd press the button, laugh really hard, catch his breath and then press the button again. He did this again and again. Watching him made me laugh.

Dan returns tonight. Days blur together when he's gone.

xxoo

To: Lisel
From: Kathleen
Date: March 11, 1997
Subj: Re: Tuesday

I've missed your notes. Let me know about this woman who is coming to look at your paintings. Sounds interesting.

I'm nervous about getting pregnant too. Nervous about being sick. My pregnancies have ground me down. I've been on my knees, begging for the vomiting to end. And I'm nervous about having another child, wondering if Sweetness really needs my entire focus.

xxoo

To: Lisel
From: Kathleen
Date: March 13, 1997
Subj: Re: Thursday

I'm thrilled your painting sold! I love it! It is truly inspired and bold. Such good news!

Mark is here visiting and he arrived today. It's great to see him.

I started writing again and it felt good. I had so much energy at the end of the day. I felt alive and clean, like I had done something that mattered. I like the work of writing. It's clean, hard work for me.

The promoting work — I imagine equivalent to you running around trying to make art slides and put together a resume — I find exhausting. But essential.

The orange blossoms are coming. You were here last year with them. Perhaps their heavenly fragrance will pull you back here again. Everything is sweet and warm.

xxoo

To: Lisel
From: Kathleen
Date: March 20, 1997
Subj: hi

We've had two glorious weeks of spring and then yesterday we jumped from the low 80s to the mid-90s and now everyone is dreading that we may have skipped spring all together. We went from heating our home to AC, in a matter of days.

I took both children to have their hair cut and the three of us swung by home, picked up the puppy and took her to the vet, where we waited for forty minutes in a small, windowless room that smelled like cats.

We're off to Del Mar tomorrow. I'm driving over with my mom and the kids and the puppy — returning next Tuesday.

That's it.

xxoo to all of you.

Written 1997
Published Tuesday, September 1, 1998
The Arizona Republic

Tricking the Tooth Fairy

BAM! I heard a door slam and I waited for someone to tattle. All was quiet. Then a door slammed again. When no one produced a hand with a missing finger, I decided all was not normal.

After searching several rooms, I found the children and the dog. Sweetness and the dog looked at me with an awareness of wrongdoing. Both children and the dog had strings of dental floss dangling from their lips. Sweetness read my suspicions. "I didn't eat it this time," he said.

Sunshine stepped up. "Mama, you don't have to worry about money anymore." She spoke with great excitement, "Daddy can work less and I can buy all the shoes I want."

I obviously was imparting too much financial stress on a 5-year-old, but I had yet to see her plan.

"We're going to make lots of money," she said. "I just need help tying stronger knots. The dental floss keeps slipping off the teeth." She was unable to contain her enthusiasm and began skipping around the room. "One dollar, one tooth," she sang. "One dollar, one tooth!"

Sweetness and the dog looked guilty and then Sweetness confessed all: "Sunshine's going to pull out all my teeth."

The neighbor boy had lost his first tooth and received a dollar from the tooth fairy. I hadn't signed up for the one-dollar-one-tooth plan. Twenty-five cents seemed fine with me. But Sunshine had been captivated by the concept of money arriving in the night. I had to agree with her it was a wonderful proposition.

And then I understood. The way she figured it, counting her teeth, her brother's teeth and the dog's teeth, she'd be rich by morning. She'd tied dental floss to individual teeth and then attached the floss to the doorknob, thus the slamming. But each time she flung the door shut, her knots came untied.

When I explained that there was a natural time to lose one's teeth, the dog looked more interested in what I had to say than either of the kids.

The next day, when the children came into the kitchen and asked for popcorn kernels, I felt relieved that they had moved beyond the drive to make money from teeth.

"We're doing a project," they announced. "We need white paint."

Sunshine and Sweetness covered the table with wax paper and spent the remainder of the afternoon painting popcorn kernels white. When they finished, Sunshine inspected all the kernels and selected two.

"This one is perfect," she said and placed it in a plastic bag. "And this one is almost perfect," she said, and gave it to her brother.

That night, both children rushed to bed an hour early. They were as excited as though it were the night before Christmas.

"Do you think she'll come?" Sunshine asked.

"Who?" I said.

"The tooth fairy," she said.

"When you lose a tooth, I'm sure she will," I said.

Then she lifted up her pillow. There on top of her floral sheets was a plastic bag with one painted popcorn kernel in it. Sunshine smiled.

The next morning, I had to rethink my position when Sunshine and Sweetness appeared dancing around the kitchen, each with a quarter in hand.

"We tricked the tooth fairy," she said as she spun and he did a jig.

Before bed that night, Sunshine showed great expectations.

"I'm concerned you've put fake teeth under your pillow again," I said, running my hand over her sheets. I would have to put an end to it.

"I didn't, mama," she said. "Don't worry." But I did worry. I worried about my deceiving her, about her deceiving the tooth fairy, about what was the right way to handle the situation. She was up to something. I just didn't know what.

When I climbed into bed that night and laid my head on my pillow, I expected silence. Instead, I heard the crinkle of plastic against plastic. I lifted my pillow. There, on my bed, was a plastic bag with one popcorn kernel painted white.

The next morning, the children appeared at my bedside.

"Look under your pillow, mama," they begged. Together we lifted my pillow and discovered a quarter.

"We tricked the tooth fairy," they sang and laughed.

"Mama, you're rich," they said. "We made you rich!"

As I watched them dance around the room, I knew they were right.

Part II

a garden

To: Lisel
From: Kathleen
Date: March 26, 1997
Subj: here I go…

Oh Lisel, here I go. My period isn't even missed yet and I've been nauseated for days! My pants won't button. You'd think someone just blew me up over the weekend, boobs, belly, cheeks and arms. My due date will be around Dec. 7th, but I've been early with the other two so I imagine this will be a Thanksgiving baby! Can you believe it????!!!!

I need to run. Sunshine just awoke. I've been up since 4:30 with nausea. Lovely.

But there is something in the air. Dan's just planted a garden and every morning and night he checks the seeds and the sprouts. He really is out there communing with the plants. It relaxes him and EVERYTHING is growing. It's all up! I teased him last night, telling him he sure has been sowing seeds everywhere. Too much really.

That's my news. Yikes, here we go!!!

xxoo

To: Lisel
From: Kathleen
Date: April 3, 1997
Subj: Re: Congrats!

Thanks for the note. Right now I feel lousy and concerned about what will happen if I continue to feed Sunshine and Sweetness white crackers and ginger ale for the next three months. At least Sunshine's been great. She went and got me a drink out of the fridge and a bowl in case I got sick. Now that's pretty convincing that all of this is worth it.

xxoo

To: Lisel
From: Kathleen
Date: April 7, 1997
Subj: Re: Monday

I was thrilled to hear from you and to hear everything is ok. I'm struggling and I can't believe how tired I am. I collapse as soon as Sweetness naps and then again as soon as the kids are in bed. I've been having terrible hot flashes all night long and night sweats — not fun, but the book says it's hormones. I'm not throwing up, but I'm still quite nauseated. I'm trying to manage this all the best I can, but at times I feel very depressed.

Glad you're doing so well. It was great to read your long note. I've felt so out of touch with you. I'm thrilled you heard the heartbeat. That's heavenly. I enjoyed hearing the heartbeat the most — it's so alive!

Love to you. xxoo

To: Lisel
From: Kathleen
Date: April 16, 1997
Subj: Wednesday

Are you feeling better today? Pregnancy has so many odd quirks. You could just be overly tired from the weekend and just need a little time to recuperate.

Well, I'm up early — before six, nauseated and trying to force feed myself before I puke. Lovely, really. I am making it through this day by day. I called a friend of mine the other day who has seen me through my last two pregnancies and I asked her how I made it because I really don't remember and she said, "minute by minute." I suspected as much. I was hoping for a better reply.

Anyway, I don't have much to say — my life is terribly uninspiring right now. If I'm not asleep, I want to be and I'm always on the verge of throwing up. I'm irritable, critical and I feel isolated. I feel like I'm in a very dark tunnel and that I have to crawl through it alone. It is worth it, but Lisel, this is a long tunnel for me.

Dan is being wonderful and it hurts his feelings that I feel alone. He's doing everything — when he can. But he still comes home late and has to go to work in the morning.

Yesterday was beautiful here. The kids played with the hose all afternoon. Thank goodness for new distractions. Well, that's enough whining from my end. I'm reluctant to write often because I have so little to say. Take care and let me know how you're doing.

xxoo

To: Lisel
From: Kathleen
Date: May 9, 1997
Subj: not much

Hi. I'm still crawling around on my knees cursing the heat and I've been throwing up more which only gets me to chew my food better. Dan and I have a joke — did you see the Terminator movies? Well, Arnold has a great line, "I'll be back." Every time I eat something, I look at it and I swear it's speaking to me with that Arnold voice saying, "I'll be back."

I agree with you on this heartbeat stuff. It is so cool. Unfortunately, my next appointment isn't for weeks. I'm more agitated about this pregnancy — worried. But I guess my only choice is to keep crawling forward and see what happens.

The best thing that happens is when I find something to laugh about. I try to laugh at least once a day. It breaks the tension in my face and body.

Sunshine is still a dream. She gets me wet rags, bowls and rose petals. Thank God for her. I feel like she is an angel sent to escort me through the tunnel. She is literally holding my hand through this.

Love to you. xxoo

Written 1995
Published Tuesday, February 10, 1998
The Arizona Republic

11 Months Pregnant

In the store window, two pregnant mannequins modeled exciting outfits. They looked fresh and alive, their cheeks flushed, their legs striding with purpose—a modern tribute to the goddesses of fertility.

Feeling dreary and green, I nibbled a cracker and adjusted the safety pin that was making an impression on my belly. The mannequins were 6-feet-2 and I stretch to make 5-feet-4. There can't be that much difference between a pregnant mannequin and a pregnant woman.

I reconsidered raiding my husband's closet one more time. I didn't know how many more days he could listen to me as I stood in front of his closet, a pile of his clothes on the floor. Every morning, I uttered the same words, "I have nothing to wear!" I don't think any man can understand the desperation in this cry. Men can only relate to the desperation they feel in not wanting to hear it repeated.

Besides, I was tired of dressing in oversized men's clothing. How many more days could I wear college T-shirts and rolled-up sweat pants? Using one safety pin to expand the waistband of pants seemed innovative; linking multiple safety pins together constituted denial. Maybe a new outfit would do the trick. I was desperate, and they had me.

I looked left, right and then sidestepped into the maternity clothing store. Instantly, I was surrounded by attractive, non-pregnant saleswomen sporting maternity wear who seemed to say, "Our clothes are so great, even women who don't have to wear them, choose to."

One brought me a glass of "chilled, mountain spring water." I was reminded of designer boutiques that wave glasses of white wine at their patrons. At that moment, I would have preferred wine, but water would have to do. Maternity clothes shopping is quite sobering.

"I'm Debbie. Let me know if you need anything." I did need a nap. I also needed assurance that someday I would be able to look at a salad with a vinaigrette dressing and not feel nauseated. And if I were really addressing needs, then I'd like when I was crying — which seemed to be several times a day — not to hear anyone mention hormones.

I thought about sharing all of this with Debbie. Instead, I said, "Thanks."

On the rack, the clothes didn't look as exciting. When I checked a few price tags, I considered leaving and visiting the nearest sporting-goods store to purchase a few pup tents to wear. Camouflage appealed to me. But then Debbie took my arm, selected a few items for me and led me to the dressing room.

"You just strap it on," Debbie said and pointed to a foam belly dangling from a clothing hook. It was pink, shaped like a dinosaur egg cut in half the long way and it had a Velcro belt.

"That's a three-month belly. Add three months to however many months pregnant you are and voilà!" She completed her sentence with the accent of a little Frenchman. "It's to give you an idea of what you'll look like."

Debbie started to leave me there in the dressing room with the belly and then she turned to say, "We also have six-month bellies."

I considered her offer for a moment. This meant, if I calculated correctly, that it was possible to see what I would look like at say, 11 months pregnant. Not that I would want to. But it was possible.

The clothes were too big without the foam belly, and with it, well, I was certain I would never get that big. I looked at myself in the mirror wearing a bra that was quickly becoming too tight, maternity underwear that covered almost all of my ribs, and a foam belly strapped around an already pregnant belly.

As a senior in high school, I had wanted my yearbook portrait to convey who I imagined I would be as an adult — I wanted an expression of thoughtfulness, maturity and beauty. Where do you see yourself in 10 years? This picture of myself in the mirror of the dressing room had not come to mind.

As I tried to rehang the foam belly on the clothing hook, I had to admit that clothes-on had been an improvement to clothes-off.

I told Debbie I'd buy the two outfits the mannequins were wearing.

Fortunately, the bag had "maternity" printed on only one side. I held the store label against my belly and, anticipating my new look, I strode out past the mannequins. Perhaps, I too, could be pregnant and look divine.

What I didn't know then — during that moment of pure delight at having something to wear — was that the dressing room was missing foam ankles, foam thighs, foam upper arms, foam breasts and a foam chin.

To: Lisel
From: Kathleen
Date: May 14, 1997
Subj: nothing

I'm excited about your June 2 appointment. What's your exact due date? Will you try to find out if it's a boy or a girl?

It's Wednesday and I'm trying to hang in there. My resiliency is waning and I'm feeling worn thin from all of this. I wonder how much longer I can hang in there. I feel like giving up but giving up doesn't make any difference — I still have to go forward regardless of how I feel about it.

I got a call today from the LA Times and they're running another piece of mine this Sunday so if you can, try to pick up a copy. Today was a good day to get a good-news call.

This is all worth it, I tell myself, ever so worth it. Are you starting to feel any movement yet? I'm really looking forward to that.

xxoo

Written 1996
Published Sunday, May 18, 1997
The Los Angeles Times

Highchair of the Decade

"**M**om?" I started. I waited until we had finished our tuna and caper sandwiches and we were cleaning up. My mother is always more reasonable after she has eaten. "Dan and I have been discussing this for quite some time." I took a deep breath and she stopped rinsing the dishes. "And we feel, that for the safety of the children…" I had made it this far. I would have to finish. "We insist that you buy a new highchair."

She resumed rinsing. "All right," she said.

"We'll pay for it," I offered, but she was gone, her mind cast back 25 years, to another house and another life. She had four children under the age of 6, two at the table, one at her breast and the other in a highchair. She boiled red beets and blended them for one child while preparing dinner for the others and my father.

The highchair had been the latest and only model available, a stainless steel tray and frame with a seat cushion the color of 5-day-old pea soup, a late 1960's classic. My parents moved twice after they purchased the highchair. The first time to a bigger house to accommodate more children. The second time years later, they took the chair along as a way of holding onto the past, something concrete that brings back sounds and smells, conversations and feelings.

My mother recalls very little of the outside world from when we all were young. She says she missed a decade. She doesn't know the music or the politics, but she can still recall what we ate. That was the decade of the highchair.

The highchair was placed in the storeroom, in the front, so that whenever we wanted anything out of the storeroom we had to first wrestle with the highchair. We never really questioned its location, but removed it and then replaced it.

But now I see its position was intentional. It was to let us know that in the depths of my mother's psyche was a woman who planned and saved for the future, someone who can't throw away a glass jar because there just might be some left-over that would fit perfectly in it. But more telling was my mother's expectation that we would bring her grandchildren, and she would be ready when they arrived. Crib, portable crib, car-bed, toys, books, booster chair, training toilet, children's spoons, bibs, and a highchair.

On the day I arrived at my mother's house with the first grandchild, my mother took out the portable crib. Dan and I got on our knees, sniffed it, flicked it, and took a knife and chipped it. We weren't certain the paint was lead-based, but we couldn't risk it. Not that our newborn could even move around yet, let alone teethe. Then we took a measuring tape and calculated that the space between the crib bars was too large. A baby could get its head stuck. We refused outright to use the portable crib.

My mother had a difficult time understanding our position. "I'll have it stripped and repainted," she suggested. But the problem of the spacing between the bars would still exist. My mother took rags and wrapped them around the bars to narrow the space.

"All four of my children slept in this bed," she said. "You slept in this bed," she said to me.

But we decided she was naïve. She had raised children without the modern parents' imagination.

When the first grandchild grew into the highchair, Dan and I agreed, both with strong reservations, to try to work with it. We stood in the driveway watching my mother spray down the highchair.

"There are spider webs all over it," I said. She took a rag and wiped them off. I recognized the rag. It had been a T-shirt of mine from summer camp when I was 9.

"Spiders could be hiding in the hollow legs," I said. She stuck the hose up each leg and water shot out of the holes.

"I don't see any spiders, dead or alive, coming out of the holes," she said.

"That's because they're too big to fit," I said.

My mother dried off the highchair and carried it inside with one hand. The tray required two hands to attach and remove, and the clamps threatened to snip off fingers of children and parents. Dan and I looked each other in the eyes and made a silent promise that we would be careful, always alert to the problem.

Then there were the remains of the highchair's plastic safety belt that had hardened and cracked apart years ago.

"You can't put children in a highchair without a belt," I said. "They can crawl out, slip out, fall out."

Before I finished my list, my mother left the kitchen and took a walk down the hall. She returned carrying an 8-foot Mexican sash and wound it round and round our daughter, securing her in the highchair.

"It works!" she said.

"What if a child is choking?" Dan whispered to me that night. "We could spend the first 10 minutes untangling the sash."

I saw his point but pressed him to try it. My mother had not fully recovered from the rejection of the portable crib. The only reason she didn't insist we use the car bed was that it was illegal.

Instead of the sash, I suggested that Dan, an engineer, figure out a quick-release safety belt. But we never came up with a better design. Meals at my parents' home always included our daughter seated in the pea-green highchair with the brightly colored Mexican sash wrapped round and round her small body. The weave of the sash became slack with use. Our daughter would begin a meal looking bound to the stake, and finish about to disappear under the tray. If it was a long meal like Thanksgiving or Christmas, someone had to retie the sash.

We bought my mother a new highchair. We selected the same model as the one we own. It's the latest design, and we had a choice of 15. My mother doesn't like the powder-blue seat with the elephants all over it. But we demonstrated the chair's features. The tray requires only one hand to slide it on and off, and the safety belt needs only a forefinger and thumb to detach a choking child.

One night, late, I muse to Dan that maybe someday we'll have grandchildren seated in our powder-blue highchair. But he disagrees with me. He says we'll be forced to buy the latest model that has a voice-activated tray and a built-in Heimlich maneuver device.

"And when our last child has out-grown our highchair," Dan goes on, "we can place it at the front of the storeroom."

I am in complete agreement.

Days later, I'm hunched over, half-inside a dark cupboard, rearranging glass jars. I'm trying to make room for an addition. I've just peeled a label off an empty mustard jar because I like the feel of the jar in the curve of my hand. I tell myself it's different than my other mustard jars because its lid is black plastic so it will resist corroding at the edges.

When I feel my back press against the top of the cupboard, I think of my mother. My posture is hers. I've seen her inside cupboards before. My hands are hers too — careful and quick with glass. And my thoughts are hers.

I'm thinking about the highchairs. Why place our powder-blue chair in the storeroom when we've finished with it and leave it to chance that my children will have significant encounters with it? I'll keep it by the back door. I'll put the pea-green one there too.

Each decade the highchairs will have a new purpose — a place to pile preschool paintings, then lunch boxes, backpacks and finally car keys. And in the depths of my children's psyches, they will know that a highchair's greatest and truest purpose is for containing and feeding small children, my grandchildren.

I fit a tall, skinny olive jar inside a pickle jar. I've made a place for the mustard jar. During this moment of elation, I realize I have become my mother.

To: Lisel
From: Kathleen
Date: May 21, 1997
Subj: Re: Tuesday

Big news — I'm able to smile again. Dan and I laughed last night for hours together and it felt wonderful. And my energy is improving. Thank God.

I heard the heartbeat for the first time and that was heavenly and reassuring!

Are you working now? I haven't heard much? Have I told you that I believe Sunshine will be an artist/ is an artist? She is obsessed with color, color relations, design, and diverse use of mediums. Do you think people are born artists? I think so. Perhaps she will stay with you some summer and see the real thing in action!

I have another piece coming out in the LA Times on Fathers' Day.

xxoo

Written 1996
Published Sunday, June 15, 1997
The Los Angeles Times

Daddy's Girl

I used to be my husband's girl. When we started our courtship in college, Dan was tan with sun-bleached curls in his hair that were always stiff with sea salt. Those were the days when he still had hair. To me he looked like Michelangelo's statue of David wearing baggy shorts, a life vest, sailing boots and sunglasses — the kind that look like purple fly eyes. Dan competed on the sailing team and after we started dating, he wished he had more time with me, but he spent every free minute he had sailing.

The sailing team was a co-ed team. They raced 14-foot boats called Flying Juniors that held one skipper and one crewmember. Often the skipper was male and the crew was female. The way the male skippers saw it, the optimal weight for the crew was 115 pounds or less. Pretty and petite was better. When I first started dating Dan, he spent every afternoon, five days a week and every weekend, sailing with a woman who weighed less than 115 pounds.

The sailors met at the gymnasium at 2:15 in the afternoon. Those people with cars hauled everyone out to the sailing center for practice. Every day Dan drove to the sailing center and back in his lemon-yellow '79 Pontiac wagon, the kind with wood panels on the sides and a rear seat that faced backwards. Dan could fit 13 team members in the car, along with all their boots and life jackets. It was the car of choice. Sometimes I'd watch them all pile in and as the wagon, clearing the pavement by only a breath, sped away, male and female limbs dangled out the windows.

I attended one sailing-team party with Dan. One boy stood on his head, drank a beer upside down and challenged a woman to do the same. She got on her hands and knees, kicked her legs in the air and started drinking. Her shirt flopped in her face. I saw her belly and the hint of her bra. I ran over and held up the shirt.

"Thanks," she said to me afterward. "I couldn't drink upside down very well with my shirt in my face."

I'd obviously been reading too many 19th century novels.

After that party, I decided I needed to learn to sail. In the summer between our sophomore and junior year, Dan and I met after work at the sailing center. We rigged a boat that had the name "Ramblin' Rose" duct-taped to the transom, and we practiced tacking and jibing.

I learned many valuable lessons that summer. You don't drop the jib sheets and let the sail luff when you smash your shin, and it is most important to remember to go to the bathroom before getting into the boat.

My hands developed hard, thick calluses and I had enough sun and salt exposure to guarantee that by 40 I would look like a shriveled island woman. But that next fall, when Dan pulled his '79 Pontiac wagon up to the curb of the gymnasium to pick up team members, I slid into the front seat next to him. While everyone else flung their arms and legs out the windows, I wrapped my arm around Dan. I was his girl and his crew.

I asked Dan to marry me several times, but he said it wasn't official until he asked me. A few months after we graduated from college, we were sitting on sand dunes overlooking the ocean. Dan was talking a lot, which isn't usual, and then, following a series of unrelated sentences, he asked me to marry him.

"Are you kidding?" I asked.

"I ask you to marry me and you don't believe me?" Dan said.

I told him he needed a ring and that he should use my full name and his when he asked me the question.

Dan made a ring out of sea grass, slid it on my finger, and asked me again, saying my full name and his, and that made it sound official. Before he finished, we were both crying. I would be his girl for eternity.

The other day, Sunshine had risen early. It was five in the morning, and we didn't have to be anywhere until nine. I suggested we make daddy breakfast. I'm always unhappy with Dan for leaving the house without eating. I can't think in the morning until I have a fried egg and a piece of toast in my stomach. Naturally, I believe everyone else is just like me.

Dan would rather sleep than eat. He sleeps until the last possible minute, shaves, showers, and then dresses while going down the hall, grabbing his keys, and heading out the door.

I poked Dan.

"Sunshine and I are making you breakfast so you should factor that in to how much time you have left to sleep."

I went back into the kitchen, set the table and poured the orange juice.

"I want to crack the egg," Sunshine said.

Sitting on the counter gave her more authority. She was taller than I was. After she cracked the eggs, I used a fork to fish out bits of shell. When I finished, I realized I didn't hear the shower running.

"Sunshine and I are making you breakfast so you should get up now," I said to Dan, who had progressed as far as my side of the bed.

When I returned to the kitchen, Sunshine had climbed down from the counter and stood with the refrigerator door open.

"We need bacon," she said.

"We're already having eggs," I said, thinking that with the bacon we would reach the recommended weekly fat allotment before 8 a.m.

"We need bacon," Sunshine said, taking out the bacon. "I get four pieces and everyone else gets two." Together we lined bacon between two paper towels on a plate.

"I want to push the button," Sunshine said. I carried her to the microwave and she pushed "2" and then "start."

"Dan, breakfast is ready," I called down the hall.

Dan came stumbling down the hall without a belt. He almost hit the doorframe when he turned into the kitchen because his eyes weren't open.

The table looked like a Norman Rockwell painting: eggs, toast, bacon, juice, newspaper. I even put the milk in a little pitcher that matches our dishes. We'd never used it before.

"Daddy," Sunshine said running to Dan. "I made you breakfast!"

"You did?" Dan said. I was surprised to hear words out of his mouth. Dan doesn't usually speak in the morning.

"I want daddy to sit next to me," Sunshine said. I quickly traded plates around and we all sat down.

Sunshine took a bite. "Mama, we need salt."

"Say 'Please,'" I suggested.

"Pleeeeeese," she said, and I rose to get salt.

Dan took a bite of eggs.

"Do you like them, daddy?" Sunshine said.

Dan opened his eyes and smiled.

"I love them, Sunshine," he said.

He never opens his eyes or smiles in the morning.

When I returned with the salt and sat down to take my first bite, Sunshine said to me, "May we please have some ketchup, mama?"

I stood again and grumbled about my egg getting cold. "Thank you for asking so nicely," I added.

Once I was absent from the table, Sunshine now confided in Dan, "I made it all especially for you, daddy."

"I love the bacon," Dan said.

"Mama didn't want to make bacon, but I opened the refrigerator and got it out and pushed the microwave buttons," Sunshine said.

"I'm glad you did," Dan said.

When we finished eating, Dan said, "Sunshine, that was the best breakfast I've had in years." This was true, because he hasn't eaten breakfast in years.

"And you know why it was the most delicious breakfast?" he said to her. "Because you made it."

Sunshine started to cry. "Thank you, daddy."

Then Dan started to cry.

While the two of them stared dreamily into each other's eyes, I cleared the dishes and scrubbed the egg pan.

To: Lisel
From: Kathleen
Date: June 4, 1997
Subj: Re: Congrats!!!!

YOU'RE HAVING A GIRL! What great news! I love girls! Girls make best friends for life. My theory, at least — whereas boys leave home and call once a week, if you're lucky. So Congrats! I love that life is always surprising!

Not much news here. I'm improving. I had a great birthday party for Sunshine — water games, pool swimming, beading and flip-flop painting with puffy paints. The kids and the parents had fun.

Sweetness just started summer school. He had a great first day and I got a migraine. That's it for now.

Loads of love. xxoo

To: Lisel
From: Kathleen
Date: June 8, 1997
Subj: Sunday

Today we celebrate my Dad's 60th birthday. All kids are in town for a party tonight at my parents' home. It's great to see my brothers and my sister with my kids. They have so much fun together. Makes me wish they lived closer.

I think I'm starting to feel movement…!

xxoo

To: Lisel
From: Kathleen
Date: July 1, 1997
Subj: my news

I fear you've left. It's only about six am here so maybe you haven't. I'll try calling. But in case you check e-mail... IT'S A BOY! My mom and Sunshine and Sweetness and Dan were all there when we saw the ultrasound... so we all found out together. It feels so comfortable for our family dynamics.... And the best news, however, was that everything looked very healthy and normal which is the biggest relief of all.

Thank goodness summer is here!

xxoo

To: Lisel
From: Kathleen
Date: August 18, 1997
Subj: There's no place like home!

Wisconsin was great for three out of four of us and I'm the odd person out. I spent ten days in a small hotel room, very pregnant, with two children, while it rained and rained, and Dan sailed and partied with our college buddies. Go figure how I managed that one as my family vacation.

The good news is — I'm home! I don't have to go back until next August and Dan is revitalized and in good spirits (this is big, given he's been so drained and run down—makes it all worth it). And Rosie survived the dog sitter.

I'm grumpy and should have waited to write you once I had taken a nap — I'm huge and with so much time left... Lisel, my thighs slap together when I walk. It's horrifying. But this is how I do pregnancy and I'm not one to not eat when I'm hungry. I do believe in trusting one's body, and my body has done a great job in the last two pregnancies of leading me through this course. Somehow it was easier living in Northern CA and believing the wisdom of the body than here in Phoenix in boob-job land. Oh well.

Sweetness ate french fries and catsup for every meal in Wisconsin. And Sunshine lived on grilled cheese. First stop this morning is the health-food store.

I didn't see Dan in Wisconsin. It was busy for him and boring for me. I knew it would be crazy, but I thought he and I would have some time, but we didn't. We spent the most time together in the car on the way to the airport yesterday.... Of course, it was pouring rain, zero visibility, many accidents — not a Sunday drive in the park. I'll bounce back. I just feel down and lonely. I really wish I had more friends here.

What a horrible e-mail! Hope you are well.

xxoo

To: Lisel
From: Kathleen
Date September 8, 1997
Subj: back to normal

I can't believe you're 33 weeks. You are truly, truly making it! Not much longer now. 33 pounds and 33 inches — I'm not far behind. I just pinch my arms and say "baby's milk." It helps me justify the soft rolls. I was at a swim gathering the other night with a woman who is 38 weeks, due soon and in a few words, a real brute. She works out every day of her pregnancy, hates children, this second one was a mistake — anyways, she looked about 3 months pregnant and had by her own admission put on a whopping 20 pounds. There are obviously very different ways of being pregnant. And of course SHE was the one who remained clothed and at poolside and I waddled about in a plaid, beach ball of a maternity swimsuit with the kids… oh well. These days, I truly appreciate those loving kind eyes, typically from much older people, who see me pregnant and say things such as "Oh how wonderful!" or "Happy, happy!" as opposed to women closer to my generation who say things like "don't you hate it when your butt gets so big?"

Sunshine started school and I love it — very crunchy — no plastic bags, no sugar in lunches and the only snacks are fruit and veggies. Her homework assignment is to turn on the porch light and draw whatever insects appear. Pretty cool stuff, but I'm feeling out of it with the moms — a lot were together at preschool. I need to get over feeling new… but I like the school. And Sweetness is starting officially tomorrow. He's really looking forward to it. We'll see how I do.

I am ready for some time for myself. The column for The Arizona Republic has been delayed and the delay makes me doubt whether I can do it or want to do it. My brain is incredibly mushy these days. I feel like I'm floating in clouds waiting for this baby to be born — it's hard to imagine making a commitment right now to think.

Dan and I are doing great. It's wonderful to be home and with him. His spirits are greatly improved after his sailing adventure, which helps us a lot.

I'm nervous about having a third child. I feel enamored with the first two and I worry about if I can keep loving with so much passion and whether I will be so blessed… crazy fears really, but more present this time than either time before.... I held a friend of mine's newborn the other day and you would have thought it was my first time handling a newborn. His poor head wouldn't stay up. It kept flopping over. My shoulder and neck cramped up trying to put the baby's head back on his shoulders. Rosie didn't know what to think of me and a baby and decided SHE was the baby and wanted up on my lap — all 80 pounds of her.

Rosie's been protesting us having left her with a dog sitter while we were in Wisconsin. She's taken to digging in the yard, chewing the children's toys and jumping on visitors.

It's hotter than hot here, and I'm ready for a break in the heat. I'm sick of all my dresses and most of the summer ones are getting too short on account of my belly protruding out so far. The front hemline keeps rising. I'm down to only a few tents that work and I don't really want to purchase a fall line of maternity wear. Ten more weeks. It's not worth it.

I've just learned I'm anemic. I'm taking loads of iron which should constipate me, then I'm instructed to take loads of Metamucil and spend lots of time on the pot....

I like thinking of you in your studio.

xxoo

A draft of a column
Written in August of 1997

First Day

Today was the first day of school for my kids. Rosie, our dog, watched me leave with the children, lunch boxes, a cricket in a jar and immunization forms. The dog knew something was up when I kept returning from the car to the house to get a show-and-tell item, grass for the cricket to snack on in the car and a release of liability form.

When Rosie really knew something was different, was when I arrived home a few hours later with no children. She looked at me as if to say, "Where's the trouble?" and then she quickly disappeared. I wondered if she could smell Sweetness's tears on my shoulder, thought something was wrong and went looking for him.

I can still hear Sweetness's words, "Mama, if you leave, I will cry." He didn't disappoint. There he was — a 2-and-a-half-year-old boy, arms outstretched with tears the size of walnuts pouring down his face, crying, "Mama, don't go. I love you."

His words linger in my heart. In fact, I'm sure he's still distraught about my not being there. Not that I want him to be. The preschool teacher said parents could call and ask the secretary to take a peek if we needed reassurance. I can't imagine Sweetness would be distracted by the red fire-truck or the plastic spiral garage. I'm certain he turned down snack time to focus on the pain of being without his mother. A half-hour earlier, I left my daughter at kindergarten. She wrapped her arms around my leg, and I had to get the teacher to help so I could leave.

Home alone, I started looking for the dog. I thought Rosie would savor the morning with me. I thought she'd nap peacefully enjoying that her tail was hers alone and not the reigns for a horse or a water-ski line. Her fur would be her own fur and not a dishtowel for syrup-covered hands or a practice beauty school for combing and scissor-clipping.

Eventually, I found Rosie with her head stuck under my daughter's bed. When I called, she wouldn't come out. I tried a bone and a ball. Then I realized that I too felt remarkably singular. My hair was still in place, the tears were dry on my shoulder and the handprints on my leg had faded. So I joined her. Together we put our heads under my daughter's bed.

I saw a Barbie shoe, a missing bikini top and Sweetness's new train that had mysteriously disappeared.

With the birth of my first child, I found that I was ill prepared for the togetherness we would experience — her burp was my burp, her restless night, my restless night. But today I feel less prepared for her school, not mine. Her friends, not mine.

I felt thrust into motherhood when the nurse handed me a newborn. "I don't know how to do this," I thought.

I have the same feeling again — with both children gone — I don't know how to do this. I know even less how to walk away, how to leave them at school. I'm the one who wants to shout, "Don't go. I love you." Instead, I cry tears the size of walnuts.

To: Lisel
From: Kathleen
Date: September 15, 1997
Subj: back to normal

Splitting headache tonight and heartburn. I've been sitting in
a parent meeting at Sunshine's new school and my belly has
been sweating on my thighs for two hours and this morning I
taught a cooking class with two other moms for fours hours to
four different classes of little kids. It's been too long of a day. I
love this school and that's most important. I've got this contract
from the Arizona Republic in front of me and my modem on
my laptop is dead. It's a sure sign that it's not time for sending
work in. I'm not into writing. I'm interviewing babysitters trying to
imagine what my needs are but I don't want to give up time with
the kids now because I'm feeling all these nesting instincts.

Glad to hear where you are — I'm close. I'm so emotional
these days about my kids. Everything makes me cry.

xxoo

To: Lisel
From: Kathleen
Date: October 2, 1997
Subj: trick or treat?

I am incredibly huge and did I tell you, I have a wart growing
on my chin? It grows visibly every day — part of pregnancy's
growth hormones. My OB says it's normal and to see a
dermatologist. Well, of course the wait to get in is four weeks
— I will finally go next week. Everyone sees it. I can see them
looking at it. I bring it up and make some joke about me being
all ready for Halloween... ha, ha. But seriously, I feel so vain,

but Lisel, it's white and cracking on the end and it will probably look like a worm by next week.

I'm not walking well anymore either and to say that I'm waddling is an understatement. A slow forward progression is my goal, but wow does it take awhile.... And I'm so grumpy. It's still over 100 degrees here. I am beyond tired of the heat and now everyone is talking about El Nino and it staying hot forever.

I paid bills late today but at least I paid them and I tried to find fabric to have some curtains made for Sweetness's room, but I got so dizzy with all the choices in the fabric store. I'm terribly indecisive. This is why Sweetness has had a pink sheet nailed to the wall to cover his window for the last two years. There were all of these women at the fabric store running around with their DKNY purses and carrying fabric swatches and talking about dining-room chairs and seat cushions. I was waddling and just trying to make some sort of forward progression. It was too much for me so I left.

Dan and I went out for coffee tonight. He listened to me blather and that felt good. Maybe I'll get better soon. But I swear my feet are going to pop, they're so swollen and tight. But this discomfort is cake compared to the nausea, so I feel small for complaining.

I'm due Dec. 3, but I expect Bongo to be born between Nov 12 and 15, if he goes the same amount of time as the other two did. You and I could end up having our babies quite close together!

Did I tell you? This baby inside of me feels like he's playing the bongo drums — he kicks all the time so I've started calling him "Bongo."

xxoo

To: Lisel
From: Kathleen
Date: October 11, 1997
Subj: Friday

I'm home at last. It's been a terrible week. I had preterm labor.
We moved to my parents' home and I had to take medicine
that was adrenaline to slow down the contractions. It made
me jitter like I'd just had 10 cups of coffee. I even had to set
an alarm every four hours and wake to take the medicine. The
cruel part was there was no way possible I could sleep the
first 2 hours on the medicine, so by the second half, I had just
fallen asleep only to be awakened by the alarm going off...
and more medicine!

I went to the hospital last Sunday morning because I was
having such severe lower back pain. I feared I was in
labor — the good news is that my cervix was closed. Now
I'm weaned off the medicine and am on partial bed-rest.
Both kids have had fevers, double ear infections, and
Sunshine has had a sinus infection. Two weeks ago — or
was it 3? Dan got that thorn in his elbow trimming trees and
everything has been in flux since then. Even the dog has
ear infections.

But today we woke at home and both kids slept through
the night and I slept for the first time in 10 days. No strong
contractions woke me. I believe we're on the mend, but it
has been an ordeal. I really feel as though I lost a week of
my life. I was getting sores on my body from having to stay
on one side or the other. Hips and shoulders parallel, my
doctor said.

I'm 32 weeks. They say I need to hold on until 35 or 36 and
that there's a big difference between a baby born now and a

baby born then. I don't feel afraid. I feel calm and that this will all be ok. I just need to lay low.

You know, I've been saying that all I want is to hold this baby in my arms, but I'm going to change my mantra, because I think sweet Bongo heard my call and I need to be patient. I couldn't agree with you more that pregnancy is a cruel state — exacting as much from the mother as possible to nourish the baby. Did I tell you I grew a wart on my chin? Growth hormones. I had to wait four weeks to get in to the dermatologist and then I was on bed-rest when my appointment arrived and I had to cancel it! I read somewhere that garlic kills warts so I'm rubbing it on my face. Ah the sweet scent of a pregnant me! But it doesn't really matter, my doctor took us off sex until I'm 37 weeks. I'm huge, with a wart on my chin, a speckled face (my pigment goes awry when pregnant) and I smell like fresh garlic. Care to dance?

Get a box ready and after you deliver that baby you can send me a tent or two…. I only have summer tents and I've busted out of one — literally popped the buttons in the back. I'm down to three dresses. I refuse to buy more maternity clothes at this point.

I read once about some French form of natural childbirth that correlated the relaxation of the mouth with the dilation of the cervix. So scream, breathe and relax those lips! Me, on the other hand, I'm tight-mouthed these days and am visualizing the ocean floor of sea anemones all closed up. To me, they look like cervixes!

xxoo

To: Lisel
From: Kathleen
Date: October 22, 1997
Subj: Wednesday

I'm pissy these days… I feel like I'm waiting and I can't do much except incubate and that feels helpless and dull and Dan's exhausted from being on double-duty and Sweetness is bored from having a mom who's on the couch and not willing to do much. But Dan said last night, this is temporary… and it will be over… I'm sure that's how he's getting through it all….

But I've got two more weeks from today that I need to hold out. I think I'll have this baby three weeks from today… that's not much time at all, except if you're carrying around 40 extra pounds and eating hormones like a box of popcorn. But a mom at school just gave me two tent dresses and I'm in heaven with something new to waddle around in. I don't remember ever waddling so much. I move so much from side to side, it is truly remarkable that I actually make any forward progress at all….

You're getting there… any day. I'm thinking of you… tons!

xxoo

To: Lisel
From: Kathleen
Date: November 13, 1997
Subj: Re: Wednesday

Dear, dear Lisel, You will make it. The first three months are hell and then everything gets better. Breast infections are the worst and are so painful. I'm sure you're doing hot compresses and breast massages — that helped me some. And drink tons of water, but so much for advice — breast infections are horrible! And newborns are tough and some are so much tougher than others. There's a huge range for how much they sleep and cry — and when they sleep less and cry more, it makes it that much harder for the mother to heal.

The hormone drop sucks too. I had one doctor explain to me that the hormone drop after pregnancy is like falling off a mountain. Nice image, huh? My solution has been to cry a lot. In fact, I think I'm trying to get ahead of my post-partum depression right now, given how inclined I am to tears!

Hang in there. It will get better, I promise. And each day does pass. Think on the bright side, somewhere around 65, we will have made it through menopause and hormone imbalances will be a thing of the past!

So much love to you! xxxooo

PS… I'm 37 weeks, yesterday. Bongo is still high, so no birth in sight. I'm still relieved to not have a premature baby. Huge here. People in stores stop and stare. I've moved from receiving the twin question to the litter question. I am going to torch my tents when I'm finished.

To: Lisel
From: Kathleen
Date: November 17, 1997
Subj: Re: Monday

I can't believe your breast infection got worse and worse and then you had to have it drained — it sounds so painful. What an entry into the second time around you've had. I am so sorry. The good news is that it seems your sweet baby is doing great. Maybe we should focus on what a great spirit she is and that we're so thankful she's here. You've been through so much, though. My thoughts are with you.

Not much here. Lots and lots of contractions, but no baby. No sleep either. I'm tired of being on the fence. Either I want the contractions to stop or I want to get the show going. This dress rehearsal stuff is a bit overdone. I'm ready.

Loads of love to you. You will get your breasts back someday. In the meantime, remember how awful it is to be where you are — it's my only consolation as a writer, that when I really suffer, it will inform my work. This is true of your painting/artwork too. You will know more as an artist because of where you are now.

xxoo

To: Lisel
From: Kathleen
Date: December 9, 1997
Subj: Re: welcome Bongo

It's been ages since I've written, I don't seem to be remembering much these days except for the number of hours I was awake in the night. My other two have been alternating night-wakings and early morning rises, so I feel that the duty of a newborn has been shared by all three of us, sort of an all-night, welcome the new baby home celebration.

But maybe things are settling down a little bit here. It just takes time. My breasts have been so engorged and are finally calming after testing the limits of my skin's elasticity. And my bottom is improving — I had a week of spasms that made labor look like a nice jog — just one of those post-labor complications.

And having a newborn is heaven, pure heaven. Except about once every twenty-four hours, Bongo projectile vomits — without any warning, only to douse himself and me completely. Lots of milk-covered clothes and sheets and pillows and chairs and carpets. And he got an eye infection from a clogged tear duct that oozed down his face. But still he is heaven. I don't know if his sweet temperament will change but the last two weeks have been tiring yet so endearing. His weight is much greater than my other two were at this age — he's nine pounds now and he can go longer between feedings. This will allow me to not feel so exhausted.

To answer your question — we don't know who he looks like. He has bits of black hair, but so did my other two and now they're blonds. His eyes were blue but seem to be darkening. He looks like my baby pictures and has funny toes like mine, but his chin and brow may be Dan's. His looks remain a constant point of discussion — everyone is claiming him as their own.

The kids are hanging in there. Very excited about the baby and yet there's more fighting between the two of them. I feel thankful to have three children and thankful to no longer be pregnant. I'm still huge and no regular clothes fit, even my big ones. I'm joyful about being able to fit into my maternity jeans again!

That's it from here. I hear Bongo waking. Loads of love to you and I'll write more when I find a minute.

xxoo

To: Lisel
From: Kathleen
Date: December 14, 1997
Subj: two and half weeks

Your e-mail gave me hope. Things sound so much better
with you. I am relieved. You sure got hit hard. Peace sounds
as though it's visiting you on brief occasions. Amen. You will
make it through Christmas. Remember the spirit of it. That's
what I'm trying to do. I want to remember that Christmas is
about new life and birth and that nothing could be more sacred
during the Christmas season than a newborn. So close that
baby is to the spirit world. So close you are as the mother, the
one bringing in the new life, an escort, if you will.

I'm driving blind right now. Sunshine is a touch sick and
Sweetness is awful, but improving after almost ten days of
a runny nose and a cough, a bad cough and a double ear
infection. Bongo has been sick, something that sends my
stress through the ceiling. First, he had an ear infection that
poured yellow gunk, the color of French mustard, and then it
moved to his nose. He couldn't nurse, so I got engorged again
(and feared a breast infection — many hot showers expressing
lumpy breasts). Anyways, he had his eye cultured and then
a few days later his nose had to be cultured…ugly infections
they're worried about.

Friday was hell. I'd been up all night with Bongo, he's coughing
too, and then Sunshine had a performance at school I couldn't
miss and she had a friend coming over…. I ended up taking
four kids to the pediatrician's office… on no nap, with huge
breasts and little patience. The doctor and I were trying to
have a serious discussion while Sunshine and Sweetness
fought over who got to spin on the swivel chair….

Bongo's on an antibiotic that made him puke the first two days, but his eye is better (was swollen shut with puss and redness) and his nose is clear enough for him to nurse. He's coughing now which makes me teary when it gets bad, you'd think I was the one hacking away. When he vomits, he's still hungry and wants to nurse again and then I'm out of milk… so we wait while my milk comes in. If the infection moves into his lungs, he goes to the hospital, but right now I think we're improving…. Friday looked bad, but today, Sunday, he seems much better. It was so sad, he was moaning a lot. It just broke my heart. Oh and he had an ear infection. Can you believe that?

But maybe we're getting there, or maybe it's just Sunday night and I've had Dan home for two days to really help out. Dan calms me, just his presence makes me feel like everything is going to be all right. Bongo is really gaining weight, up to 9lbs 3oz — that's a good sign that he's doing well, but I'm still tense. That's an understatement.

I hate having sick babies, Lisel. I did this with Sweetness and it was hell. There is nothing worse to me. I just exist with a knot in my stomach. I'm tired but won't admit it easily and push on, not having much choice. But these times pass and I hold onto the moments with the kids. There are dear moments right now when Sunshine holds Bongo sleeping in her arms, when Sweetness makes a painting to go over the changing table to help Bongo feel better — and Sweetness is hacking away with a cough and a double ear infection — a lot of love here right now, so I am deeply thankful for that.

Peace.

xxoo

To: Lisel
From: Kathleen
Date: December 19, 1997
Subj: hi

I sent you a long e-mail the other day, but it somehow got erased. I saved it somewhere else so I'll re-enter it when I have time. Bongo has been sick and in and out of the pediatrician's office. Monday night he crashed — fever, refusal to nurse, lots of coughing and rapid breathing. Tuesday morning we raced to the doctor's office where Bongo turned blue during a coughing fit. They put oxygen on him and then sent us to the hospital in an ambulance. He was diagnosed with RSV, a terrible virus for infants, and put on IV antibiotics, oxygen and breathing treatments every two hours around the clock. The treatment included suctioning which meant putting a catheter down his nose and throat to suction out mucus. Horrible, yet very helpful in getting him to breathe better. The kids moved into my mom's, and Dan and my mom orchestrated life with them while I was on around-the-clock duty at the hospital. I went for four days without going outside. I didn't even leave my room.

We were released this morning and are spending the weekend at my mom's — a sort of halfway house. Bongo's still quite sick, but out of danger and in need of breathing treatments that I administer (minus the suctioning) around the clock. My breasts are still a mess, I'm sure you know better than I — but I've been pumping with the hospital electric pump to try to relieve the engorgement — and I got sick and didn't sleep for days — an hour here and an hour there — never more than three and a half hours in a 24-hour time frame. But each day he improves, and my spirits improve with him.

It broke my heart trying to hold him with all his wires attached. We were attached to all of these beeping machines that sounded alarms at any movement.... And the hospital was overflowing, packed beyond capacity....

But I am home. Well, not quite, I'm home at my mom's. I'm sick, did I say that? Achy all over and coughing but I'm out. I felt like someone a century ago who had a contagious disease and was sent to a TB ward with all of these people and babies packed in and hacking away... God it was hell. But we made it out. And I pray to God Bongo didn't catch anything else that was there. Part of his right upper lung collapsed from the mucus. That's stressful, but it will heal and he looks so much better now. But Lisel, I'm in shock and I'm thankful and I want to cry — that will come.

I missed my kids so much, worried about them so much, and now that I'm with them again, I don't have any patience and I'm wiped out... a day or two of sleep should help.

Love to you.

xxoo

Written 1998
Published Tuesday, December 22, 1998
The Arizona Republic

Sliding Curtains

A hospital cleaning crew scrubbed the vinyl La-Z-Boy, wrapped crib sheets in plastic bags and scoured the bedside table, the sink, even the closet knobs.

When the workers finished, they were ready for the next patient, but I wasn't. A sliding curtain separated me and my baby from the other half of the room. I liked having a few hours alone. I could imagine my newborn Bongo and I were in the maternity wing again, a few floors down on an elevator. It had been a mistake, how sick he was, all the tubes and monitors attached to my 2-week-old baby. I let myself think we would be going home soon, maybe even in time for Christmas. It was all I wanted, that, and to see my other children again.

I had left them in a hurry. Not really saying good-bye, I pushed my mother-in-law at them while they ate their cereal. "I'm taking your brother to the pediatrician. I'll be back," I said and raced out the door. But days passed and I hadn't come back.

Bongo had RSV, a common cold for adults, a virus that can kill an infant. During the night, Bongo's lungs had filled with mucus and he couldn't breathe well. I counted his breaths at 90 to 110 per minute. Normal is below 60.

His ribs sucked in hard for air, the skin wrapped around each bone. He was still so new to me that I felt in awe of his having come with ribs. When I called the receptionist at the pediatrician's office early that morning and told her about Bongo's ribs, she said to come immediately.

"He's retracting," she said. It was the first in a long series of medical terms I would learn in a short period of time.

I was at the pediatrician's office with Bongo when he turned blue. The doctor slapped an oxygen mask on Bongo's face and his natural color returned. It would be months before my natural color returned. I wanted to believe children are not returnable, that they've been stamped "ALL SALES FINAL." But that's a hard belief to hold on to when you're racing down the centerline in an ambulance, sirens blazing, heading back to the hospital. But I held fast. This baby was mine, and we would go home again.

A nurse interrupted my thoughts and told me I would be getting a transfer patient from the intensive care unit as my next roommate.

"Can I unplug their TV and you'll tell them it's broken?" I asked. I couldn't take any more confessional daytime talk shows. The next patient would invade the room, another child with RSV accompanied by relatives carrying balloons, flowers, tuna casseroles and bags of clothes. On the other side of the curtain, I'd have both breasts hooked up to an electric breast pump because Bongo couldn't nurse.

My next roommate must have arrived in the middle of one of Bongo's breathing treatments because I didn't hear anyone come in. Every two hours, a respiration therapist came to our room to give Bongo a breathing treatment. It involved misting medicine into his breath intake, pounding his chest, front, back, and sides and then running a tube down his nose and throat to suction out mucus. Bongo screamed throughout the treatments, and I helped the respiration therapist pin him down. The treatments were what would make him better. I told myself this each time. When the respiration therapist finished with us, she went to the new child. This is how I knew they were there.

From the cry, I could tell the infant was a boy, and older than Bongo. I guessed he was 7 or 8 months old. As the respiration therapist pounded and suctioned, I heard his mother's voice, "Calma. Está bien. Calma. Está bien." When the respiration therapist left, I heard the mother whispering and patting her child, "Mi nino, mi nino." Her voice was tender. I felt calmed having her there.

The first time I saw the mother, she walked past me to use the bathroom. She was younger than I imagined; her voice had sounded so strong. Her hair fell past her waist. It was thick and rich and brown. On her way back to her side of the curtain, she stopped in front of the sink. I could see her reflection in the mirror. She flipped all of her hair over her head and used both hands to twist it. In an instant, her hair was pulled tight into a knot behind her head. She splashed water on her face, took a breath and returned to her child.

When my mother came to visit me, she slid back the curtain and spoke with the woman in Spanish. We learned that the mother and her child had been air-evacuated from a rural town. "Yo pense que mi nino era muerto," the mother said. She had thought her child was dead. But the doctors had been able to revive him. She had arrived at the hospital with no extra clothes, no money, and no family near by.

It was an eight-hour drive to her home, and her husband couldn't get off work to see her.

My mother asked the woman if she had eaten.

"No," the mother said. We learned that it had been days since she had eaten. Because she wasn't considered a patient, she wasn't given a food tray.

"Necesitas comer." my mother said.

My mother had brought me a bag of food and offered the woman hard-boiled eggs, oranges, and bread. Together the woman and I peeled hard-boiled eggs, dipped them into piles of salt and ate them. Then we peeled oranges. When we finished the oranges, we ate a loaf of banana bread. Together, this woman and I passed that night and the next several days. When the respiration therapist came, the screaming and the suctioning began with Bongo and ended with her child. Then we had a quiet hour, before the routine began again.

To calm Bongo, I sang to him. My father sent me words from a church camp song he had learned years ago. It was a Welsh folk song, and I imagined a mother a long time ago singing this song. I learned the words: "Sleep my child and peace attend thee, all through the night. Guardian angels God will send thee, all through the night... I my loving vigil keeping, all through the night." I sang. I cried. I prayed. On the other side of the curtain, I could hear the mother whispering her songs, wiping her tears, and holding her silent prayers.

The next morning, the mother got great news. They were going home.

She slid open the sliding curtain. "Ya nos vamos," she said. "Dile a tu mama muchas gracias por la comeda. Buena suerte! Adios."

She told me she was going, asked me to thank my mother for the food, wished me good luck and said goodbye.

When the cleaning crew came to scrub down her side of the room, I was sorry she was gone, and that night, I missed her. The next morning, my pediatrician woke me. He was making early morning rounds. It was still dark outside. Bongo's breathing rate had come down and he was able to breathe room air again.

"How would you like to take your baby home for Christmas?" my doctor asked me.

I looked at Bongo in the plastic hospital bassinet. "We would love to go home for Christmas," I said. While the doctor put in the discharge orders, I phoned my husband. "Come get us," I said. "He's going to be OK. He's going to be OK." I wanted to see my husband. I wanted a shower. I wanted to hold my children. So eager was I to leave behind the sickness, the buzzing of the machines, the relentless pace.

But I still hear the metal rings sliding on the curtain rod in a hospital room. Someone pulls the institutional fabric shut, to try to make suffering private, but there on the other side of the curtain is a mother singing to a sick child in the middle of the night.

"Calma. Está bien. Calma. Está bien."

our holiday letter

December 1997

Dear Friends,

Finally, it feels as though we've settled into life in Arizona. Our biggest news is that our dear Bongo was born November 26, the day before Thanksgiving. Since his birth, I have had a deep sense of completion and thanks. I feel as though my family has finally arrived and I no longer have to serve as a transportation vessel.

Sunshine, age 5, has as much spunk as usual and has taken to attaching colorful strings to her hair. Sweetness, now 3, is upset he's not going to school every day with his sister. He is quite the talker and very empathetic. I had weeks of false labor contractions, and one morning, Sweetness wobbled into the kitchen clutching his waist. "Sweetness, are you all right?" we asked. And then he moaned, "I was awake all night with contractions."

Dan is still in the yogurt and smoothie business. And I still call myself a writer, although I didn't write much this year.

We wish you smooth sailing for 1998.

Much Love,

Kathleen, Dan, Sunshine, Sweetness and Bongo

To: Lisel
From: Kathleen
Date: April 4, 1998
Subj: we're back

I've really missed hearing from you. We're regrouping today.
Dan's home. We're going to weed the garden, grocery shop,
pay bills and try to appreciate how normal and straightforward
life can be. I feel like the last several months have been
blinding, Lisel. How anyone survives motherhood is beyond
me. I suppose it is all ok when I go at it day by day, but the
cumulative picture is overwhelming.

xxoo

Written 1998
Published Tuesday, May 11, 1999
The Arizona Republic

Women and Chocolate

There were only two raspberry chocolates left in the chocolate box that was hidden on top of my refrigerator. This doesn't sound like a problem, but it was for me, because my mother doesn't like raspberry chocolates.

It began when I asked my husband to buy me chocolates for my birthday. He didn't. To his credit, he gave me a pair of Italian sunglasses. But sunglasses don't speak to my mother and me the same way chocolates do.

My mother claims that when there are chocolates in her house, they call to her — no matter where she has hidden them. This is why she doesn't allow herself to keep chocolate in her house very often. "It gets in my mind," my mother says about chocolate, "and then it becomes too much of a distraction."

I told myself I would receive a box of chocolates for my birthday. When I didn't, I couldn't get chocolates off my mind. I felt owed. I spent an entire week feeling sorry for myself, and then I drove myself to the candy store. Never in my life had I purchased a box of chocolates for myself.

An older woman wearing a white dress and plastic gloves followed my instructions. I read labels and pointed to my favorites. I did pick two chocolate raspberry truffles for my husband and several chocolates my mother adores. As difficult as it is to share chocolate, she and I always do. It's our way of showing each other how strong our love is.

As the woman packed my half-pound box piece by piece, I saw that, rather than waiting for a man to buy me chocolates, I could do it myself, at will or even at whim. I felt this awakening could shift the power dramatically in male-female relations. The information felt dangerous.

When I arrived home, I hid the chocolates on top of the refrigerator from my children and my husband. They do not know how to make a box last. I told only my mother where I had hidden the chocolates. Unlike sunglasses, with chocolates, you never have to ask where you've put them.

"We're feeling neglected," the chocolates call to me if I've been absent too long. "We like attention," they coo when I open the lid for a second time in an afternoon.

I was out of town when I telephoned my parents. "The chocolates at your house are calling to your mother," my father told me. My mother and I didn't know whether chocolates at my house would be able to speak to her. Now we knew.

"Tell her to go over and take some," I said, feeling generous.

"Friends don't take friends' chocolate when they're out of town," my mother said. My mother has her rules and she follows them. When I arrived home, I checked my chocolates. They were all there, and my mother felt honorable.

About the time of my birthday, I lost my babysitter and I was forced to call upon my mother in moments of crisis to take care of the baby. When I asked, she would hesitate, check her date book, and, if she could, she would rearrange her schedule to accommodate mine.

The first time I went to pick up the baby at my mother's, I brought her a piece of chocolate to say thank you. I left it on her kitchen counter.

"Did you leave this for me?" my mother said on the telephone. She knew I was the only family member currently in possession of chocolate.

"Of course, I did," I said, "To say thank you for babysitting."

The next time I asked her to babysit, she didn't hesitate. The third time I asked she said, "I'd love to." When I went to pick up the baby, I brought my mother two pieces of chocolate to say thank you.

"You know I'm going to salivate the next time you ask me to babysit," my mother said to me as I was leaving.

The next day she called me, "How are your interviews with sitters going?" I told her my stories of no-shows, late-shows, and the one who canceled because she didn't want to be stressed trying to get to her yoga class on time.

"That's too bad," she said. "I'll babysit for you today if you need me." That's when I knew I had power over my mother. The trouble was my chocolate box was getting low. I tried to ask for my mother's help only in emergencies. Even then, my chocolate ration had dwindled. There were only raspberry truffles left and my mother and I don't like them. My dilemma was whether to purchase another box of chocolates to keep my mother babysitting for me. I agonized over the decision.

And then I wondered how long could I ask my mother for favors and leave pieces of chocolate on her kitchen counter as a thank you? It might be interesting to try to find out, I reasoned.

My mother's birthday was approaching. I returned to the candy store. The same older woman helped me. When the woman asked, "Is this a gift?" I paused. I wanted to do the right thing, but with one box of chocolates, I would lose my stand-in babysitter and set my mother free. Was this really what I wanted? I liked having my mother call and ask how she could help me. I could keep the chocolates, take them home, put them on top of my refrigerator and I'd have help for a month. I could reduce my mother to one piece per babysitting period and make the box last two months.

"Yes," I heard myself say. "It's a birthday present." I watched the woman wrap the box in colorful paper. That evening, when my mother saw the shape of the box and the gift-wrap, she knew the contents immediately.

"Now I have my own," she said with delight. She sniffed the box, held it close to her ear, and I could hear the chocolates whispering to her. Then she carried them down the hall and didn't tell me where she hid them.

I went back to my house and peeled off the outside chocolate coating on the raspberry truffles and ate it. Then I searched my chocolate box. Finding only wrappers, I had to accept that the box was empty. I sat for a moment in silence and then I began to hear voices. I was alone in my house with an empty box of chocolates, but my mother was in her house with a full box of chocolates.

I called my mother. "I'm going to the store, do you need anything?" I offered.

"Let me get my list," she said. And I knew she had me.

To: Lisel
From: Kathleen
Date: April 29, 1998
Subj: Re: Tuesday again

I have so much news for you! We're buying a home!
We're moving in two weeks — it's across the street from
my parents' home. It's our dream house — well, it will be
eventually. We've been looking for a couple of years for an
older home (1950s) that has never been remodeled, on a
big lot, and we found it, moved on it and voilà! I should have
known that when you were moving that I'd be moving soon!
Doesn't it seem that way?

We'll live at my parents' for a month or so while we fix up
this old house — the total remodel will have to wait. I'm in
the middle of boxes and had the same thought you wrote
about — I'm literally moving boxes from this house that I never
unpacked (it's been almost four years). The question arises —
is this stuff really essential?

xxoo

Written 1998
Published Tuesday, June 16, 1998
The Arizona Republic

Papa's Parade

My father strides into his kitchen and gestures to a room filled with boxes. He's wearing gray sweats and running shoes. Over the noise of three children, the TV, my husband, my mother and me, he pronounces, "This isn't a mess, these are my grandchildren." He laughs a deep laugh.

My mother and I are trying to make my refrigerator items fit into her refrigerator. Neither one of us can throw away a sesame teriyaki marinade we might use someday. We lined her counter with ketchup bottle to ketchup bottle, mayonnaise to mayonnaise, jelly to jelly.

We've been at my parents' home for one week. We were planning on selling our house and then fixing up our new house. My parents suggested we move in with them temporarily. Maybe the idea slipped from their lips before they could hold it back, but I accepted.

"How will you handle living with your mother?" friends asked with concern.

"Easy," I said with confidence. I didn't even think about living with my father.

"Papa," the children scream to my father.

"Eat," I say to two of them. I assure myself that it's not that uncommon for grown children to move back home. For centuries, generations of families lived together — often in one room. Here, we might as well be living in one room because we all stay in the kitchen.

"Would you like a surprise?" Papa asks the children.

They know not to deny him. Sunshine purrs, "Of course. Anything will be fun because it's with Papa." My father gets rosy from her admiration.

"Ah, Sunshine and Sweetness," he says. "I love having both of you here." Tears fill his eyes. In my life, I have never seen him cry.

Later, my mother realizes that amid the confusion, he left his vitamins on the table and took her estrogen instead. Perhaps this is why he is emotional.

"When you finish, it's time for a parade." Papa takes sugar and cinnamon and pours spoonfuls on their toast. The children cheer. He redirects my disapproving glance to show me that they ate the crust.

After the children lick the sugar from their plates, Papa swoops Sunshine up in one arm and Sweetness up in the other. He starts marching and singing to the tune of "Seventy-Six Trombones" from the musical "The Music Man." My father doesn't know how to sing without clapping, stomping and dancing. His kettle on the stove starts whistling for him to make his tea. My mother and I exchange looks — as if this man needs caffeine.

He bounces the kids like a lid boiling on a pot — up, down, up down — around the house and then he pauses for a moment in front of a surreal painting that has two ladders going up into the clouds. "Here's the painting of *Ladders to Heaven*." Then he marches onward to a Nativity scene and he stops for a moment of reverence. "There's baby Jesus." Everyone is quiet.

With one loud stomp, the mood shifts on the beat, and the parade is on again. He sings and then stops to point out two nude statues. "And there are the naked ladies!" Papa looks at me to catch my reaction. I raise my eyebrow at him. My seriousness only encourages my father.

"Here's another naked lady," he says, glancing my way, eager to get a response.

I imagine my son coming home from preschool with his drawings and the teacher's handwriting underneath. Rather than, "This is my dog, Rosie," the words read, "These are naked ladies."

"Papa," I say with disapproval.

The next time my father circles the room, he modifies his song. To the tune of "Seventy-Six Trombones" he sings, "Ladders to heaven, baby Jesus, can't say it. Your mother will get mad!" And the children chime in, "Can't say it!" They repeat their new song as he marches and they bounce. The walls spin and the floor rocks.

After my father leaves for work, we're all woozy. Sweetness keeps circling the room singing, "Ladders to heaven, baby Jesus, can't say it!" Recovering from a morning with Papa is like walking on land with sea legs.

When Sweetness sits down for lunch, he finally stops humming and for a long time he's quiet and doesn't eat. I think maybe he's still dizzy. And then Sweetness says, "I figured it all out." His facial expression is serious for a 3-year-old. I stop eating. My mother stops eating.

"If you climb up the ladders to heaven," Sweetness pauses, "then you get to the baby Jesus."

My mother and I look at each other, relieved. At least he didn't say that when you climb up the ladders to heaven you get to the naked ladies.

To: Lisel
From: Kathleen
Date: May 4, 1998
Subj: Re: Sunday

My sister is here to help me with moving and play with the kids. She and I spent more time talking than anything else. Maybe that's why she came.

Did I tell you I am in love? When the older two are at school and I'm home, I spend hours kissing Bongo, especially his belly. He laughs and laughs and I bury my head in the crook of his neck and smell his skin and fat and he laughs again. I feel as though I have everything I want in life, everything. My life is so full right now. I feel deeply blessed.

The children are well today and life is warm. Kisses. xxoo

Written 1998
Published Tuesday, December 1, 1998
The Arizona Republic

Ketchup or Mustard?

When I was pregnant with my first child, I'd sit in a wicker chair, feel the baby kicking, and dreamily, I'd wonder what color to paint the nursery. Not that we were going to have a nursery. We lived in a one-bedroom apartment, but people asked and so I gave color selection my consideration. It seemed important.

By the time I was pregnant with my third child, I didn't worry about what was coming. I worried about *who* was coming. I used to think children were born alike and that parents made the difference. Then I saw my first two change me more than I could ever hope to change them.

The more my third baby flipped and kicked inside of me, the more I feared his arrival. Before my baby was born, I said to my husband, "This one must have come from your side." My husband's family gets irritable if they're not moving. My family doesn't have that problem. Most of us would rather own a mountain bike than ride one. I'm starting to believe each person is born with a set personality and it's possible to inherit it.

To determine which genetic lineage my children lean toward, we discovered the ketchup-mustard test. A preference for mustard means they follow me. A willingness to eat anything bathed in ketchup means they follow my husband. Mustards talk; ketchups prefer the weather channel. Mustards jay walk; ketchups cross at the light. Mustards think 10 minutes late is on time: ketchups argue there's a difference. Mustards believe they're right; ketchups usually are.

Immediately, after my third child Bongo was born, I wanted to know who had arrived. The day Bongo ate a cold, veggie burger covered in ketchup, I knew. I just didn't know the extent of his inability to discriminate. My first two children never put things in their mouths. I'd say to them, "No, no, no," and dutifully, they'd resist. Then I had Bongo.

"No, no, no," I'd say to Bongo and then he'd tilt his head, give me a four-toothed smile and shove the dog ball into his mouth as if to say, "Full throttle ahead on that immune system."

The day Bongo started to crawl, my life changed. For months, he must have sat on the kitchen floor eyeing the newspaper, the phone cord, the dead cricket and bemoaning, "If I could get these feet and hands to coordinate...oh what a day, what a day that will be!" The way he saw it, mobility could only increase his menu selection.

The trouble is that Bongo likes to explore the far reaches of the house gathering what he perceives are edible samplings. Every time I turn to put pasta in a bowl or tie a shoe, Bongo is gone. I run frantically around the house calling, "Where's Bongo? Where's Bongo?" I don't like losing babies.

Usually, my daughter finds him in a corner, teething on a dog bone or behind a potted plant, eating soil. I tell myself that he'll end up an expert at gardening. He'll dab soil to his tongue, "Too acidic, needs Epsom salt mixed in, then these roses will bloom." Something positive has to come from his taste-tests.

At soccer practice the other afternoon, Bongo sat so still on the sidelines, watching the girls play ball. It was a peaceful moment until I noticed Bongo chewing and chewing and chewing. When I swiped my finger in his mouth, I expected the usual rock or leaf. Instead, I found chewed chewing gum.

Can you imagine the 911 operator?

"There's a crazy mother on the line, she's screaming, says something about her son chewing gum."

"Is he choking?"

"No," I'd say. "But I am."

Another day, Bongo was missing. I checked the pantry first. He likes playing in the garbage there, but the door was closed like it's supposed to be. I checked the bathroom, then the dog bowl. I heard noises in the pantry. Bongo must have crawled in and shut the door behind him. He was already covering his tracks. I feared the worst. When I saw the wastebasket but no Bongo, I felt relieved. I could hear cooing and babbling, and I knew he was fine. I looked behind the door. There was Bongo teething on the toilet plunger. He was perfectly happy until I screamed, and then he cried.

For about an hour after I put Bongo down for a nap, I get panic attacks that he's missing. "Where's Bongo?" I cry out and then I assure myself he's in his crib. Sometimes I tiptoe into his room to verify he's sleeping. "Relax," I tell myself, "He's safe." I feel incredulous that this child who terrorizes when awake can look so angelic asleep.

What I've learned is that I can't change my children. I've tried. They're given to me at birth, who they are. All I can do is help them figure that out by giving them options. I have to believe someone put a paintbrush in Monet's hand, and it was most likely his mother. But I wonder if she drove him to soccer practice for years before giving up and handing him a brush.

"If you're going to stand there and look at the field, at least paint it."

Every night, I sit in my wicker chair and pray Bongo and I will make it through another day. Now I know it's not about paint color. It's more about the paintbrush. And, with a little ketchup, Bongo would probably eat it.

our holiday letter

December 1, 1998

Dear Friends,

Hello. This year, we don't have much news. I'm still writing a regular column for the paper, and Dan's still pushing smoothies. We sold our house and bought the one across the street from my parents. We moved in with my parents while we planned a remodel. Six months have passed and we haven't started construction. I have to think if my mother stopped cooking, we might move out sooner.

Bongo is now one and climbing. He stands on the fireplace hearth in diapers and dances to Elvis. He prefers power outlets over toys; dog food over human food. He's already had athlete's foot. One week after he started walking, he dribbled a soccer ball down the sidelines. We like to think we should videotape him for his World Cup debut. This is how we make ourselves feel better about all of his adventures, believing that someday they will add up to something positive.

Sweetness is 4. He likes school, conversation, trains, and digging. Despite his new independence, he still insists on someone lying down with him every night while he falls asleep. Always, Sweetness tosses a tired arm over me, to keep me from leaving before he's asleep. "I will always love you," he whispers. I tell myself to hold on to the moment because I've yet to meet a grown man capable of such pure devotion.

Sunshine, at age 6-and-a-half, finally has two loose teeth. From my perspective, she has arrived. I believe Sunshine was born wanting to be 6-years-old. She has elaborate plans to build a treehouse in two fig trees at our new house. She's been selling lemonade to raise money for supplies. I was concerned when a mother at school approached me and told me her daughter wanted to give all of her savings to Sunshine for the treehouse.

I've had some of my worst moments this year. Sweetness has been challenging the reign of his sister, especially in the car when she's buckled in and I'm driving. All I can do is count, "One, Two, Three…" This is not about time-outs, it is about the number of Beanie Babies I will acquire upon arriving home. Once home, the children run, hiding stuffed animals while I scream, "Seven, I need seven Beanie Babies, or else I'll choose." Cruella couldn't do a better job. The children offer up ones the dog has chewed. "Accept these mama, and we won't fight again."

It is on this thought that I'll end. Wishing you a happy holiday season, we send our warmest love,

Kathleen, Dan, Sunshine, Sweetness and Bongo

Written 1998
Published Tuesday, January 19, 1999
The Arizona Republic

Treehouse

Our house has two old fig trees. Together they form a leafy, dark canopy over the earth. In summer, during the hottest days, it's still cool under the fig trees. Sunshine and Sweetness would sit with their backs against the trunk, eat figs and discuss tree limbs. It was there in the low branches that they wanted to build a treehouse.

I always have had legitimate excuses to offer my children, explaining why right now wasn't the best time to stop and build a treehouse—I chose to pay bills, wash clothes or make dinner instead.

While on vacation at the beach, Sunshine and Sweetness held a lemonade sale to raise money to buy supplies to build the treehouse. The children quickly learned that people in swimsuits don't carry change. So any person in street clothes who was walking on the beach was seen as a potential customer and was accosted by my children.

"Lemonade for sale," Sweetness yelled. He circled the beach walkers with a misspelled sign. "Pink or yellow?" he asked. The children could spot a person with a backpack from half a mile down the beach.

"We're raising money to build a treehouse," Sunshine told two men in street clothes who had decide to buy lemonade. When the men heard about the treehouse, they dug in their pockets for extra change. One opened his wallet, and a badge flashed. The children exchanged a look of reverence. He was a police officer. Dropping a dollar in their jar, he paid double for the lemonade.

After the officers left, Sunshine decided sharing her treehouse plans with customers was a good selling point. "We're raising money to build a treehouse," she said again and again. Each time, adults paused. While she poured lemonade, the customers searched their pockets as if to buy time to linger in the past.

In the fall, Sunshine drew floor plans for her treehouse at school, and she invited friends to share ideas. She promised it would be large enough for all of them. They would leave their homes and sleep in the treehouse. She called it a secret club and told everyone about it.

One mother at school pulled me aside: "My daughter wanted to bring all of her savings to school to give to your daughter." I laughed nervously. "For the treehouse?" I asked. The mother nodded and then suggested we could shop for supplies together and I agreed.

Then Sunshine's class began a unit studying trees. They counted trees, drew trees, read about trees. Sunshine used phone books to press leaves between waxed paper.

"Fig leaves are beautiful," she said. "Yes," I noted, relieved we'd completed yet another homework assignment.

"We have to build the treehouse soon," Sunshine said to me one day. "People at school are starting to think it won't happen." I stopped what I was doing. "Yes," I said. "Soon."

The next homework assignment asked each child to talk with an adult about a tree that was special to them and then to ask the adult to write comments. The question took me back to age 6, my daughter's age. We lived on a mountain, and our backyard opened to a desert. In a dry river wash, there was a Palo Verde tree. In its shade, the earth was damp, and four or five blades of grass grew. My friend Sara and I called it Little Green Valley. We gathered quartz rocks and encircled the grass.

I asked Sunshine's teacher if I could read other parents' responses. As I read through them, I saw glimpses into sacred spaces. It was like reading old love letters. There were stories of climbing trees, of carving in trees, of swinging from trees, of bones being broken falling from trees. Trees provided private time, away from adults, to eat fresh fruit, to watch squirrels, to make unreal worlds real. One father had a fallen tree that he played in with his brothers. To them, it became a fort, a rocket, a submarine. Another parent loved a cherry tree in the middle of her garden and raced against birds to eat the ripest cherries. No cherry has ever tasted so sweet, she wrote. It seemed no memory could be as sweet as those that adults have of trees.

I realized this was something I needed to give my children, as important as dinner or clean clothes. I walked out to the fig trees to try to imagine how to begin building a treehouse for my children. The fig trees were without leaves. Through the skeleton branches, I saw a rusted ladder propped against the base of the trunk. In the fork of the tree, there were slats of wood and a tin can. Inside the container, I found tangerines and pecans, a ration.

Tired of asking, or waiting for help and not having help arrive, my children had built their own treehouse. When I climbed the ladder, I remembered how comforting it is to sit in a tree's branches, eat fruit and let life be.

our holiday letter

December 1, 1999

Dear Friends,

Hello. Last year, I wrote that we were living with my parents while we remodeled a house across the street from them. To our surprise, we're still living with my parents. They only laugh. When we finish, they plan to remodel and move in with us. How could we ever say no?

Sunshine is 7. She's into building secret forts outside with her friends, writing letters to her friends, and talking on the phone with her friends. We argue over how long is long enough for a phone visit. Several times, I've overheard her say to Sweetness, "Don't interrupt. I'll be off in a minute and then I will listen."

When asked what he loves to do most in life, Sweetness, age 5, called out, "Gardening!" He likes anything that involves a shovel, dirt and his Dad. He has his own gang of friends where he escapes his sister's domain. Together they build spaceships out of Legos for hours. He's particularly interested in good guys, bad guys, the glory of battle and the gore of defeat. On good days, he's willing to build bad-guy ships and let his brother act as official destroyer.

Bongo is 2 and determined to find a nut that fits perfectly up his nose. He has found pine nuts to be too small and get lodged too deeply. He has found pistachio nuts too large and stretch nostril skin. Blue playdough rolled up like a small nut is his preferred option. A year later and Bongo still turns everything he finds into a drum. He flipped over the child-potty, and pounded on it. "Drum!" he said. Hoping to redirect his musical inclinations, we gave him a miniature guitar for his birthday. He strummed the strings, flipped it over and pounded on it. "Drum!" he said. The other day, I found him hitting the fish tank with a stick. "Drum!" he said. The fish swam in circles. Proud of himself, he said, "Fish dance!"

So that's a bit of life here. We wish you a joyful holiday and a Happy New Year.

We send our love,

Kathleen, Dan, Sunshine, Sweetness and Bongo

Part III

delphiniums

a diary entry

December 29, 1999

Today we learned that my mother has a form of cancer they believe is treatable.

My mom's doctor from Tucson said to us, "I'm very optimistic and I never give up."

My mom was sitting on a gurney before she started her first chemo treatment.

"Oh good," my mom said, "I'm going to get to see more grandchildren."

a letter

Written in December of 1999

Dear Francie,

Words don't often fail me, but I must say I'm somewhat at a loss to express my concern for you. I'm sure you think a thousand thoughts a day and feel the whole range of emotions every day as well. I hope the outpouring of genuine love and affection we all feel for you will help to buoy your spirits.

You have been such a stalwart and loving caregiver. It's hard for tough moms and wives to be down — at least more than 24 hours! I suggest that you enjoy the rare opportunity to be on the receiving end of all that care — knowing you, you will be standing at the kitchen sink or reading a story in no time at all!

Take care and lots of love,

Mary

a note included with flowers

Written in December of 1999

Francie,

Espero que pronto se recupere.
    Love,

Maria

a diary entry

January 20, 2000

Today Bongo ate mouse poisoning and my mom lost all of her hair.

I was on the phone with poison-control, picking blue chalk out of Bongo's molars while my mom pulled clumps of brown hair off her red sweater.

Later when we knew Bongo was all right, my mom showed us her new wig and Bongo ran to the dress-up box and put on the blue clown wig. He wanted her to know that he had a wig too and then my dad picked up Bongo and started singing "Zippity-Do-Da" and parading him around the kitchen singing about it being a wonderful day.

I don't agree.

a card

Written in January of 2000

Dear Francie,

We hope you're feeling better today. We know you've begun chemo and hope you're handling it as well as you could expect. Keeping you in our very good thoughts and sending you many prayers.

Love,

Lynne

a postcard from Uncle Phil

Postmarked 2000

(Uncle Phil is my Aunt Mary Lou's husband.)

Francie,

A 3-legged dog walks into a saloon in the old west. He saddles up to the bar and announces, "I'm looking for the man who shot my paw."

Love,

Phil

To: Lisel
From: Kathleen
Date: February 21, 2000
Subj: hi

I've wanted to write you but didn't take the time. Things have been quite hard here. My mom was very sick for months and was misdiagnosed as having irritable bowel syndrome. She had tremendous abdominal pain and she was losing a pound a week. In December, she had emergency surgery for an obstructed bowel and they found a large, cancerous tumor and removed what they could. We later learned that she has an advanced stage of uterine cancer. We now have a wonderful doctor in Tucson who is one of the best in the country for gynecological cancers and he is overseeing her care.

She has been through three chemos and has one more and then she will have surgery in March to see what's left of the cancer and to reattach her bowels — she's had an ilyostomy, a bag, because the intestines were so damaged.

Since the original diagnosis, all of our incremental news has been good. The cancer is contained within the abdominal cavity and has not spread to the lungs or bones or liver. The chemo is working well to get rid of the cancer. She looks better than she has in a year, but it has been stunning.

It's been a lot Lisel. Thank God we're still living with my mom and dad. The children add so much to the overall good nature and humor of the home. Meals still have to be made, singing still has to happen. Dancing too. Life has this incredible poignancy to me right now where each day is raw and real and memorable.

Our home should be ready in 6 weeks or so, but I want to make certain that I get my mom through the next surgery before we move out. We may delay our move-in date — but something else is bound to postpone it without my intervention.

It's been tough on the kids, but I'm doing my best. My mom improves each day from the December surgery — so that helps, but the chemo treatments are hell. But today we're in the middle — 10 days to go before her next chemo and I'm enjoying the lightness around the house.

I send you my love, as always, and oodles of kisses to your sweet girls.

To: Lisel
From: Kathleen
Date: March 1, 2000
Subj: hi

I'm low energy today. I think I'm sick but I have no intention of admitting it. Tomorrow we go to Tucson for my mom's last chemo before surgery. It's tough because she always seems to be feeling so well just before it's time to go and get zapped again. But she is doing well so I don't want to complain.

a diary entry

March 26, 2000

2nd Surgery, Day 6 in hospital

Bathing my mother —
Feet, toes
Towels on the floor
Light
on her
naked body
Blue cap on her head
I said to my mom, "You're like one of my kids."
My mom said to me, "Moms become kids."

To: Lisel
From: Kathleen
Date: May 17, 2000
Subj: oh my

God I feel like I could use a week of therapy, then a week of drinking, dancing and smoking to deal with the therapy and then a week at a spa to clean out my system from the week dealing with the therapy. Do I sound like a mess? I am. I'm fried, frazzled, teeth-clenching and I've even caught myself twisting a candy wrapper again and again because it felt good.

Too much going on and not enough process time, sane time, dance time, sex time, bath time, naptime. Definitely on the edge. I'm worn down right now, very thin. Dan's gone, which throws off my sense of balance. We've moved stuff into our home and I want to be living there, but my mom is not well and she's asked me to stay here. I have been, but I can't. I can't anymore. I need out. I need space. I need to be sane. I need a break. But my mom, who is proud and strong, came right out and said, "I need you." What do I do? What do I do?

The kids are all ending school right now and I cry every time I think of saying good-bye to their teachers because I've had three incredible women step up to bat for me this year. They loved my kids so well when I couldn't be there to do it, and I knew my kids were in strong, caring hands. I feel grateful for these women. They have done so much for me.

That's it. What I would give to have you next door.

Please tell me I'll make it. My mom is going to wear the beautiful wrap you gave me at my sister's wedding in June. Thank you for such a lovely gift. It was her last, unresolved clothing stress for the wedding.

a card

Written in the spring of 2000

Hi Francie,

Hope you're hanging in there. Sometimes it seems that feeling "the way we used to" will be impossible. 2 surgeries in one year (or less) really knocks it out of you – even you! We think of you always and know that you'll be bouncing back in no time (that's a relative term!)

We've made plans and hotel reservations for *The Wedding* — can't wait. Let me know if I can do anything now — or at the wedding site. Feeling useful is what I do best! Being useful is even better.

Take care — be a patient patient! The overall report is so wonderful!

xxoo

Mary

A draft of a column
Written June 24, 2000

The Second Dance

My mother danced at my sister's wedding. The Big Band music was fast and fun, ready for a celebration. When Francie stepped out onto the dance floor, the crowd cheered. The groom held her hand and eased her into the rhythm. They rocked side to side. Francie talked and forced a smile. Slowly, the groom forgot his concerns about my mom and let himself be led by the saxophone. He spun Francie once and then again and again because that's what the music asked for, that's what life asked for.

Francie followed the groom's lead and let herself be twirled. Each surprise spin made her laugh. She looked beautiful dancing. But then the groom tried a fancy move. His arms and Francie's were crossed and held up towards the twinkling lights. I saw the groom's arms reach high, black tuxedo sleeves stretching, white shirt cuffs exposed. Time froze while my mom and I waited to see if his arms would clear her wig.

For months, my mother had nightmares that her wig would be knocked off at my sister's wedding while dancing with a man other than my father.

She and I had considered adhesive spray, the kind my daughter uses on art projects. But my mom worried her head might itch at the wedding if we covered it with glue before she put on her wig. As it was, the elastic lining of the wig irritated the base of my mom's neck and so we stuffed the wig with a silk scarf to make the wig tolerable.

"I'll have to wear a wig at my daughter's wedding," Francie said to the woman in the pink chemo lounge chair next to hers. It was my mother's first chemotherapy treatment. In three weeks, she would lose all of her hair.

"But you'll *be* there," the woman said.

Whenever my mom started to worry, she and I both said, "But you'll *be* there," and the worrying stopped.

When the beat of the music changed, the groom's arms cleared my mom's head by four inches and time started again. Francie spun out of the tangled embrace, wig intact.

A groom in a rented tuxedo was swept away by the music and danced Francie back to the rhythm. She remembered that there is music, there is dancing, there is a rhythm to life that is hers alone, hers to find and lose and re-find. The night began again, and so did Francie's life.

a diary entry

Written in early November of 2000

Sweetness just turned six. He sat at breakfast eating his cereal. Sweetness counts everything, he thinks in numbers. "Mom," he said and took another bite. "How many chemos has Francie had?" I thought about it. "I'm not sure," I said. And then he asked, "When will Francie have her last chemo?" Sweetness is our child who can speak what is written on our hearts. And I had to answer, "I don't know," but she was at his birthday serving cake.

a diary entry

Written in late November of 2000

The night before my mother went in for her fourth surgery, Sunshine, age 8-and-a-half, said, "Let's have a show!" Sunshine put on a leotard, a fancy skirt and started doing cartwheels in the family room. I played the piano and my father, Sweetness and Bongo made instruments from paper towel rolls and marched around the house singing. My mom and Dan were the audience. There is something profound about partying into the night.

To: Mark
From: Kathleen
Date: December 12, 2000
Subj: hi

There's no walk in my life, no movement. It all feels frozen, waiting, waiting as one does, holding breath, not willing to exhale, for fear that even the slightest movement of air might shift the outcome.

I watch as my mom navigates barefoot across a floor of broken glass. I can't walk with her, can't throw her shoes, or bandages or wings. All I can do is witness her walk, the pain, the triumphs, the fears. And pray that she holds faith that it's worth trying.

There is my father, a bit late because of a line in the hotel shop. He was purchasing sunblock. He sits down next to my mother and they clink glasses. "Cheers," he says. His eyes are tired from the stress but his face is calm.

He has looked at life without her and he knows that the ocean breeze is more sensuous because of the bends it took to navigate the curves in my mother's legs. He feels the breeze on his face and it reminds him that he has skin, that he is alive.

our holiday letter

December 2000

Dear Friends,

Hello. After two years of living with my parents, we moved into our house in May. Our remodel was finally complete. We'd been sleeping five in two rooms — six if you count the dog. As soon as we moved in, the children posted signs on their freshly painted doors, "Kepe Owt, Nok First." We were all happy to have space.

But at night, footsteps padded down the hall to our room. The sitting area where Dan and I imagined sipping wine and playing cribbage was taken over by a pool raft, a sleeping bag and a child. It wasn't long before the entire room was scattered with mattresses, stuffed animals, and children's books. Now our bedroom looks like a daycare center and we awake to the scent of wet diapers, dog breath and stale milk. Not much for romance, but it does feel like home.

Sunshine is Sunshine is Sunshine. She's into lime green. Her room is lime green. Her jacket and shoes are lime green. In her lunch, she prefers key-lime yogurt. At 8-and-a-half, she has an abundance of artistic flair and creativity. She's started writing her own stories revealing an ease for storytelling and drama. She's into photography and secret codes. During a science demonstration at school, she used a mirror and Morse code to spell a message. The boys in her class erupted when they decoded the dots and dashes… "Girls Rule!"

Sweetness is 6 and in kindergarten. He loves having his own homework, lunch box and water bottle. He's having a wonderful time, because in his words, "My sister already taught me everything." In Sweetness's free time, he builds elaborate Lego vehicles that traverse the universe avoiding all contact with Bongo. The new house has given Sweetness a great deal of outdoor work to do and he loves helping Dan move dirt, trim trees and haul clippings.

Bongo is 3 and quite social. While riding in the car, he insists, "Roll down my window, mama!" At stoplights he shouts to the closest person, "Hey, what's your name?" The startled person answers and Bongo responds, "I'm Bongo!" When the light turns green, he yells, "See you next summer!" Bongo is still obsessed with drums. Kitchen pans, paper towel rolls, chopsticks — anything he can make into a noisy instrument, he does. Then he commands, "March, NOW!" and we're off, banging and clanging.

Last December, Dan made some noise of his own and left the yogurt/smoothie business to start a software company designed to help food manufacturers. He has a group of seven, packed into an office above a Chinese restaurant and a Pizza joint. He works late nights and boasts that in three minutes and twelve seconds, he can purchase a slice of pizza and return to his desk. Even though there's a dartboard and fishing pictures on the office wall, Dan assures me they're making great progress and occasionally brings home a demo on a handheld device to prove it.

Recently, I've been working on several children's books. The work is fun, but sporadic. I've been more focused on my mother. She has had some pretty serious health concerns. She's doing OK, but like any ongoing medical problem, she has good days and hard days. Overall, things look positive and we think everything is going to turn out well.

I've been especially thankful for the kids this year. Despite the difficulty of the day, we continue to have tea parties, build forts and dance around the house blowing on toilet paper rolls.

We send our love,

Kathleen, Dan, Sunshine, Sweetness and Bongo

To: Lisel
From: Kathleen
Date: December 29, 2000
Subj: hi

I have myself tucked away in my closet. Two children play
Monopoly with a sitter while the other one pretends to nap. I
am proud to report that I survived another Christmas — even
despite the fact that my children took turns holding an all-night
vigil Christmas Eve. They took turns waking me. "It must be
time to open presents!" I'll be the one in the photos this year
who is hunched over with gray circles under my eyes — but
I'm smiling. There remains still — despite all the plastic —
something magical about Christmas.

I am writing to you now, in part, because this Christmas, more
than any other, I have been keenly aware of the blessings of
my life. You are dear to me — in so many ways. But this year
you hung in there with me — and for that I am grateful.

Again, we find ourselves in the middle of an intense time with
my mother. She had an emergency surgery in November and
is now undergoing a combination treatment — radiation 5 x's a
week, chemo 1 x a week for six weeks.

Sometimes I feel afraid. But I try to stay up and hold hope for
her. I walk each morning. I pass my mother's roses. I see a
particularly beautiful white one. My mother has told me several
times that I can pick roses from her garden for my home. This
white rose has bits of hot pink on the ends of each petal — as
if someone dunked it upside down into an empty paint bucket.
The color reminds me of my mother.

I do not pick a rose. Every now and then the roses here can
bloom all winter. The sun is warm on my face as I return home.
Maybe, just maybe, this will be one of those winters.

To: Lisel
From: Kathleen
Date: February 9, 2001
Subj: hi

I have to tell you I have never felt so sad in all my life. My mother is all right, but I don't know if I am. I pull it together for the children. Thank God for the children. How I love the early morning with them because I am not alone. Always there is some warm body that has crawled into my bed, and as I lay there awake I can feel Bongo's heart beating. Or Sweetness's hair against my face. Or Sunshine who is all beauty, all joy.

My mom's treatment continues. Her spirits are up. She enjoys and savors life more than ever before. Her frantic busy self seems to have disappeared. She's often relaxed and joyful. She makes the extra effort to help Sunshine gather rocks outside for a rock collection and to review Sweetness's homework on vehicles. She tells him a story about her father working on train cars to install the first refrigerator cars.

But her skin has a frightening uniformity to it. There are no visible veins — they're all dried up from the chemo. Her eyes are bright but when her platelet count gets low, she gets dark, heavy circles under her eyes and bruises from the slightest bump. Her memory goes too. She tells me the same story three times in an afternoon. The chemo makes her jittery. Sometimes she just fades and I notice her quiet, seated on the barstool, white. I pour her water, put lemon in it. I give her food, food she can eat, white bread and meat. Her stomach can't tolerate anything else.

Yesterday my mother was sitting on a barstool in my kitchen.

"There's some drug they can give you to protect the intestines during radiation," my mother said to me…but the boys were fighting in the playroom.

"What happened before he hit you?" I asked Bongo who said, "I bit him." The story unfolded and eventually they agreed to take turns and I returned to the kitchen.

"But you don't have to have radiation again?" I asked.

"Oh, no," my mom said, "This is just in case." She just finished six weeks of radiation treatment, five times a week and chemo one time a week.

And then Sunshine came in and started to practice the piano.

"What song is that?" my mother asked. She's tone deaf.

"Mary Had a Little Lamb," I said.

"Oh, I hear it now," my mother said.

Sunshine played the song again and my mother asked again, "What song is she playing?"

"Mary Had a Little Lamb," I said.

"I can't tell," my mother said. "That's why I was never any use to you all when you were practicing. You could play whatever you wanted and I couldn't tell."

"But you did make us practice," I said to her.

"That's true," she said.

I took piano lessons for ten years. I can barely read music, but I can sit and do something everyday. I attribute the discipline of writing to my mother making me practice the piano.

Later, my mother sat with the boys on her lap and Sunshine stood at her side. They were looking at the music book my mother had brought over as a gift. My mother is a scientist, tone deaf, but determined to pass on to her grandchildren a love of music.

I was in the kitchen trying to wash lettuce, scrub potatoes and brown meat. But I was flattened by the radiation oncologist. Yesterday, I went with my mother to her last radiation appointment to take her to lunch afterwards to celebrate that she had made it, that she was done.

My mother had her final treatment. We had questions to ask and then we had to decide where to go for lunch. My mother weighed herself. She had gained weight during radiation and she cheered and so did the nurse. This was a victory, but then we saw the doctor. He was complacent, resigned, heavy. His arms were crossed on his chest, resting on his belly.

There were lab results on his desk.

"Your blood marker levels are too high. You still have cancer active in your body. A lot of cancer."

Afterwards, my mother was visibly shaken. She drove, then pulled over and stopped in a parking lot. She ran her hands over her face, through her thin hair. "Oh, gee," she said. "Oh, gee."

But later she said, "I'm letting it go."

I was up all night composing angry letters to the doctor.

But there was my mother, children on her lap, pointing to the instruments saying, "This is an oboe. This is a flute."

a diary entry
March 1, 2001

I remember our first family trip to the Grand Canyon. I was surprised the US Government hadn't run a protective fence around the entire perimeter of the canyon, so dangerous and exposed the edges felt. As I stood there at the top of the canyon, with a straight drop in front of me, I had a keen awareness of the dirt underneath my feet. Looking down made me dizzy and I longed for a guardrail. It would be like standing at Niagara Falls but without the railing. Land, water. But with the canyon, it was land and no land. Ground to stand on, and no ground. Step and misstep. Life, death. The Grand Canyon was too big to fence. You have to look at the edges. You feel the edges.

Living with someone who has cancer is like that, it's like walking along the edge of the Grand Canyon — it's breathtaking, so beautiful, because one's mortality is so present.

The preciousness of life is defined by its edges.

A draft of a column
Written March 30, 2001

Blow That Horn!

My mom insisted on taking Bongo to hear the symphony rehearse. Bongo is 3-and-a-half and thinks he's the Music Man. He wears a plastic bandleader hat and marches around the house with a wooden spoon, beating on pots and pans, bowls and buckets.

My mom called ahead and received permission from the conductor to bring her grandson to watch the orchestra practice. My mom and Bongo entered through the stage door. When they arrived, the musicians were tuning up. Bongo saw the tuba and asked if he could touch it. The tuba player said yes. When Bongo reached out and touched the instrument, the tuba player surprised Bongo and blasted a long, low note. My mom was holding Bongo's hand. She said he was so excited by the sound, he trembled. She said she could feel his heart racing and he was speechless.

Together my mom and Bongo went upstairs and sat in the front row of the balcony.

When the symphony started to play, Bongo leaned forward and yelled, "Mama Francie, Mama Francie, look! There's a bassoon! There's a bassoon!"

Later my mom said, "He knew every single instrument."

And I knew who had taught him.

If I had death in my sights, what special things would I do with the people I love? What would I insist I do? And then I wonder, why I don't live this way all the time, with a sense of purpose and urgency, of getting every ride in before the fairgrounds close?

If my mom doesn't make it into my son's memory, I can tell him that on her 59th birthday, she took you to the symphony. You were 3-and-a-half and you touched the tuba. For days afterwards, you went up to everyone you met and said, "Hey, I touched the tuba!"

That same night my mother learned that her blood marker had gone up even higher. That her cancer was really back. But when she sat down to her birthday dinner at our house, she retold the story of taking Bongo to the symphony.

"I'm so happy I took him," she said.

Does it have to take cancer to make us know that life is for loving and that nothing else matters, nothing?

a postcard from Uncle Phil

Postmarked 2001

Francie,

BUMPER STICKER:
THERE ARE ONLY 3 KINDS OF PEOPLE — THOSE
THAT CAN COUNT AND THOSE THAT CAN'T

Love,

Phil

To: Mark
From: Kathleen
Date: June 14, 2001
Subj: hey

You were right. You called everything. Dan did come around.
I felt so bad for saying I couldn't take him leaving right now on
a fishing trip — like I was pathetic. But somehow your e-mail
this morning helps me put all of this in perspective. I need him
here and I am sorry his fishing trip doesn't work this weekend,
but there will be other times.

He was sorry for hurting my feelings and for ranting. And he
was great about it last night. We're both just pretty stressed
and it's the long-term stress which wears on one.

My mom seems a little better. The CAT scan didn't show
anything awful — the absence of bad news. Her blood marker
is roughly the same. Down a tiny bit. She has chemo today
and tomorrow. Maybe it's working.

She was so dear last night. My dad brought her over to my
house. It was a beautiful night. There was a breeze and it was
cool. The kids were outside playing and she and I sat on the
lounge chairs. (It was a big deal that she walked that far.) She
put her hand on mine and told me bits of good news about
herself.

a diary entry

Written in the spring of 2001

Today, my mom said to me, "I've decided to make my time with people I don't know count. I've learned all the women in the labs' names and I compliment them on their jewelry. Women always like the jewelry they're wearing. Eventually, I draw them out. I want that connection. I know they're alive. I want them to see that I'm alive. That I was here."

To: Mark
From: Kathleen
Date: June 15, 2001
Subj: hey

Boy am I wiped. It made me nauseated just driving my mom
to chemo today. She was tired, didn't sleep well last night. The
chemo wired her, or maybe it was the steroid that wired her.
Anyways, she wanted to sleep at chemo so I'm going back in a
few hours to join her.

Dan just called. He and I are really struggling through this
time. Thank God he's sweet, or has a sweet side. He's trying.
Bless him for that. But this is tough going.

To: Mark
From: Kathleen
Date: June 26, 2001
Subj: hi

Yesterday, we finally had a break in the heat. It rained. The kids
and I skipped swim practice and played outside in the rain for
hours. We all piled on the hammock and felt the storm wind blow
through us and then we rode our bikes around the neighborhood
in the rain and then on to Wendy's for frosties and fries.

My mom's cancer marker is coming way down — from the
high 80s to the mid 30s. This means she's finally on a chemo
combination that is working. I'm glad for that. But it seems
the complications don't stop. She has a massive infection in
one foot and it's spreading. We're hoping the antibiotic kicks
in soon. But she's elated about the news. Her needle in her
port came out this past weekend and she was able to go in the
ocean in Del Mar. She was thrilled. On top of the world!

a card

Written in June of 2001

Dear Francie,

Who would have ever thought low protein markers could make your day??? I am so happy to hear such incredibly good news!!!

So to celebrate . . .

> just a little treat
> that I'm not sure you can eat
> to help you see
> through that deep black sea
> the light at the end of the tunnel . . .

(I never was a decent poet...)

And if the chocolates can't sit and wait until you can eat them with abandon, I hear that they make great barter material for favors —

Francie, I hope you are having a wonderful day. I think the absolute world of you.

Love and hugs,

Sharon

To: Mark
From: Kathleen
Date: September 19, 2001
Subj: hi

It's Wednesday morning. Glad to have made it past a week
after last Tuesday. My mom had a rough day yesterday —
she's in the hospital now. A CAT scan on Monday revealed
a large cyst on her abdomen. It was drained yesterday. I
am hopeful that she will have some relief today and that the
pressure of it is gone. She was in great discomfort. Maybe
today will be better for her.

I am off to shower, to school, to the farmer's market and
then the hospital. I love the nurses on my mom's floor. Some
oncology nurses are the absolute best. Absolute. These
women glow. They laugh, tell good jokes, are kind, gentle and
not afraid of death. They know that as long as a patient is alive
what they do matters and sometimes it matters a lot.

To: Mark
From: Kathleen
Date: September 20, 2001
Subj: hi

It's Thursday here and I'm home, not going to the hospital today. I probably shouldn't have gone yesterday — I was getting a migraine. I still have it. I am going to curl up in my bed, under the covers and find heaven in the darkness. This computer screen is even too bright.

I'm trying hard to focus on good things and things that make me smile, but I'm sad. My mom dodged three bullets headed for her, at least temporarily. She had several procedures two days ago and is doing much better today… maybe her major discomforts have been reduced. That's all good. But it looks like all of this could drag on for a long time. Maybe she'll keep improving.

To fight the good fight is to try to resist the fear and the sorrow, but it's been a couple of really intense days. We didn't know if the procedures done on Tuesday were going to work. It was really, really scary. It's gruesome. I don't want to tell you the details because they were hard enough to live once.

It's hard to watch my mom suffer. I can't do it, even though I know she's going to be better today. I'm still in desperate need of a break. I'm home and I'm going to get in bed and curl up in a ball, probably hold one of the kids' blankies.

I miss my life. I miss laughing easily and playing with the kids and making love and I even miss folding laundry. I miss working in my office at my computer and the sounds of my fingers on the keys. I miss talking to friends about everyday life and not holding back. I am so unwilling to horrify with stories of what my days are like right now.

Ok, enough. I'm off to bed.

a postcard from Uncle Phil

Postmarked 2001

Francie,

If a man is standing in the middle of the forest and there is no woman around to hear him, is he still wrong?

Love,

Phil

To: Mark
From: Kathleen
Date: September 23, 2001
Subj: hi

It's Sunday night and we're still in a fog here. It seems like
the suffering will go on forever. I remember the first time I
was in labor and it went on forever. No one ever told me that
when the baby was born, the pain would end. This time feels
remarkably similar. I try to remind myself that the feeling that
suffering will go on forever is part of the nature of this time
period and not the nature of all of life. Wind will come from
a different direction someday and the sights and scents will
change.

But right now I am half-crazy. Crazy when I am not at the
hospital with my mother. Crazy when I am there with her.
No one place feels whole. I feel divided, internally between
worlds, as if part of me is trying, futile as it may be, to go with
her. Mama, will you wait for me? You always said you'd never
leave without me. You were always the mother who waited,
while I tied my shoe, while I combed my hair, while I made one
last phone call or changed my shirt, and then later, you were
there helping me tie shoes, burp babies, change diapers. And
yet, now it seems she and I will separate. How a child does
this when there is a cord is beyond me.

My heart seems to break and then heal only to let itself be torn
in two again.

a letter to my mom
Written October 10, 2001

Dear Mom,

Since you and dad seem unable or unwilling, I don't know which it is, to discuss the possibility that you might die soon, I have decided to write you a letter.

I thought there was nothing left to say. It seems you and I have spent a significant portion of our waking hours on the phone with each other talking. You know I love you. You know I love you dearly and deeply. And I know you love me. This clearly isn't one of those letters that has to tell you that.

Perhaps this is what makes losing you so hard, is that I do adore you, that I have savored you, that I do know how good I have it. I am aware of how much I have, having you as my mother.

There are so many things I won't lose when you go. There is such goodness and grit to you that it can't help but be passed on. There is a beauty and order about you that makes the world more harmonious for me. I look for beauty and know when I have seen it because of you, because it is so you to surround yourself in beauty.

But I am most sad about things I will miss. I will miss you most profoundly at the beach. I love the girl-time we've had there. When we shop and cook and walk and swim and take care of babies. I like sitting in the living room with you and talking about people as they walk by. I will miss you there.

I will miss telling you stories about the children — the good ones and the worrisome ones. I will miss fretting with you about them. I will miss being able to call you when Dan is grumpy and I just need someone to listen.

I'll miss you at dinnertime, when the light is getting soft and the day is on its final glow. That time of day always reminds me of you, you telling me about being a little girl and playing in neighbors' yards, not wanting to come home — me playing in neighbors' yards and you asking me to come home — my children playing in your yard and me asking them to come home. There is a lingering there.

I will miss you when my first play is performed. I will trust, if at all possible, you will find a way to navigate through the spirit world to be there. I expect that. And I will be able to know. But I'll still miss your voice telling me how wonderful it is. You have always, always, been my most ardent and loyal fan. I am profoundly grateful for your faith in me. I do crazy things I would never have dreamed of because of the simple reason — my mom thinks I can.

So thank you, thank you for believing in me, for pushing me to work hard, for asking for excellence and for enjoying my work when it's done. Thank you.

I'm sure there's so much more. But my tears are cried out for now. I don't know when you're going, none of us can say, but these are things I want you to know.

All of my love,

Kathleen

To: Ali
From: Kathleen
Date: October 29, 2001
Subj: hi

Not really an e-mail, but I'll say it anyways, only because I have a headache and I'm tired of talking. Chemo isn't working. Disease declared drug-resistant. My mom told there's nothing else they can do. Put on pain meds. New goal: keep her comfortable. But even lots of narcotics don't help. Now people weep and call and line up to see her. My dad sleeps at the hospital. My siblings fly into and out of town, again and again. My fridge is empty. Produce rots. And yet, my children put on Halloween costumes and dance around the kitchen. Thank God for children.

Some moments my heart breaks. Others I am strong and I feel my feet and the earth and see the moon rise and the sun set and I know it is good to be alive. And then I am numb and I hear nothing, not even a child, my child, tugging at me, telling me the same words again and again, louder and louder and still I hear nothing. I want to make love because I can feel and then I weep because I am alive and there is nothing I can do to stop time, to hold time still. And why would I want to? To prolong her agony, to delay the inevitable? Yes, that's why I'd want to. One more day to hear the cadence of her voice tell me how to turn the orchid in the vase so that it contrasts properly against the color of the hospital room wall. So she suffers, but I garner one more memory, one more flavor, familiar, most familiar, but a favorite — an action, a gesture, in the present, because I can. Greedy me.

Then something shifts and I'm angry, furious. Why her? Why me? Why now? I see an old woman in the room next to hers and I think yes, this is appropriate. I wanted decades more. Decades. Now I'm grasping for days, days that seem stolen. Days suffered for. And all I want to do is scream, "No!" As if that would stop an incoming tide.

All I am left with is the image of me on my knees in the wet sand with waves breaking in front of me, water up to my waist and I'm weeping.

Days, weeks, months, no one knows. No one knows how sweet life is, until it's almost gone.

a diary entry
Written October 30, 2001

On Saturday night, I learned that my mother would die soon and I sat on a barstool in the dark in my kitchen and cried. I thought the children were in bed and that I could sit and cry alone. There, around the corner, came Sweetness wearing his long, white nightshirt. He crawled onto my lap and then he started talking.

"Mama, I know why you are crying," he said to me. "Daddy told me Mama Francie is very sick. It's OK to be sad."

With his kindness, I cried harder and then he kept talking.

"I know you're sad and it's OK to be sad, but when Francie dies her spirit won't die. It's just the body that dies. Not the important stuff. The spirit stays. Most of Francie doesn't die, just the body stuff goes."

I rocked him in my arms. After a while he spoke more. "It's OK to be sad and to miss her, but you will be with her again. And mom, you'll be happy again. You will. Just work on remembering times with Francie that you had before she was sick. Remember when you were a little girl and she took care of you and you had lots of happy times together. You'll feel better."

With tears streaming down my cheeks onto Sweetness's hair, I said, "You are golden Sweetness. Pure gold."

"I won't forget Francie, mom. I'll tell stories and you'll tell stories and we'll remember her. I'll never forget her." And then he hugged me.

We sat there as one, a mother holding a child, a child holding a mother.

To: Ali
From: Kathleen
Date: October 31, 2001
Subj: hi

Today I asked my mom to plan her own memorial party. I was terrified of bringing it up, terrified more of missing the opportunity to bring it up.

"Mom, what are your favorite flowers? What flowers do you want?" I asked it.

"Delphiniums. I thought you'd ask." She smiled. "The incandescent blue ones, the ones I get at the beach. They die quickly, don't last long. I suppose that doesn't matter." She smiled, laughing at her own joke. "But they're even beautiful when they're gone. I love the blue petals when they fall on the table, the color is beautiful." And she waved a hand about slowly in the air, showing petals falling.

As I left the hospital room, I turned to look back. As the door was closing, I could see my mother, a hand waving.

Petals falling.

a diary entry

Written in November of 2001

The other day at the hospital, my mom told me stories from when she was in college. She took flying lessons and eventually earned her pilot's license.

She was sitting up in the hospital bed, but she was looking back — smiling.

"I loved flying. I mean I really loved flying," she said. "I flew a two-seater, a Piper Cub. I'd top off the gas tank and then I'd take off and stay up for as long as I could. I'd watch my gas gauge and I'd keep flying. I'd fly and fly and fly and then I'd bring her in on empty."

To: Ali
From: Kathleen
Date: November 1, 2001
Subj: hi

I am naked, wearing only a towel, and I have to go be a mom. Dan is out of town. I have kids to get ready. I have wet hair and all I want to do is write to you. I have a nine o'clock haircut. I'm tired of hacking away at my own bangs and having it look right one minute and uneven the next.

Yesterday was one hundred days all in one. News broke around town about my mother's impending death. Dear, old friends came to see my mom and tell her goodbye, to tell her what and how much she had meant to them…. It was one story of love after the next.

And my children, I took them to say goodbye. It was the first lucid day my mom has had in weeks…. I can't write about it.

It was the day of tears. Even the seamstress at the alteration store wept when she asked about my mother and I told her…. My mom and I have been going to see the same seamstress for years. And the nurses wept and the teachers at school and the parents in the parking lot…. My dad in the kitchen at 7 AM weeping. Sunshine in my arms weeping. My brother on the phone in tears.

It is the most beautiful sight to see so much love and a woman who gets to hear it.

Worst motherhood moment: at the elevator, trying to leave the hospital. Sunshine sobbing. Sweetness white and in shock, and Bongo hyper (regressing to head-banging and jumping off vinyl couches). Bongo put his hand on the elevator door as it was opening and his fingers got stuck between the door and the wall. He was screaming and all I could think was — at least we're at the hospital. Finally, with pure mother strength, I pulled his hand out.

Superman should have been a mother.

We stopped on three different couches trying to make it to the parking lot… after Halloween and the sugar and the lack of sleep and the tears… heaven help me.

There is more, but I can't write it. I feel it's urgent to write so I have it. But I usually find my way back.

On duty.

a letter

Written November 1, 2001

Dearest Francie,

It seems it is time to say our goodbyes. Certainly not what I had looked forward to doing together at this point in our lives.

Kathleen tells me your spirit is strong, your attitude positive. This, my dear, does not surprise me. As ever, you are a model for us all.

Please know how much I have enjoyed renewing our early, original friendship. And Richard considers himself very fortunate to know you. You are not only great fun, but, among other things, always bring significant ideas to our discussions. Both so valuable. Like <u>you</u>. You are appreciated <u>and</u> <u>loved</u>. Thank you for all the time together.

A very loving goodbye.

Merrilee

a card

Postmarked November 1, 2001

My dearest Francie,

You have the ability to spread such glowing light on the lives of so many. We are all made better people by your presence. What a gracious, loving, intelligent, compassionate person you are.

Thank you for the gift of your being.

God bless you.

Regina

a card

Postmarked November 1, 2001

Dearest Francie,

We will treasure, forever, so many memories we have had with you. We will never forget you, dear friend — thank you for sharing your life with us and giving us your beautiful smile and warm, loving heart.

God's blessings and our love,

Jeanne and Gary

a letter

November 1, 2001

Dearest Francie,

At a time of separation, words seem inadequate; but words must do. We hope they will express in part the deeper feeling of love and appreciation we feel for you.

Our families have shared 40 years of companionship and experiences. We raised our children together; shared holidays; traveled from beaches to the mountains. Through all these experiences you have been an inspiration and a delight.

You have been the driving force that kept the Book Club going and our minds from growing old and lazy. You have been the consummate hostess and have given us countless memories of good times with friends.

We have shared with you so many happy times — and a few bumps in the road. You took the good times and the bumpy roads, both in stride and with equanimity. You have been the best of friends. You have been an inspiration during these past two years, leading the way and showing us how to meet death with courage and dignity. We love you. We will never be fully separate from you; your spirit and memory will always be with us.

Kay and Gary

To: Ali
From: Kathleen
Date: November 5, 2001
Subj: hi

I'm up early and it feels like a good day here. I wake, not crying but with hope. Delusional as I may be, I hold hope. It feels sweet and good.

It is sacred time here. As my mother grows thinner, she seems to purify. She sleeps more, but her awake hour is so lucid. She is more here than she has been in months. Although her body is being starved right now, no food intake, no IV food, so is the cancer. Somewhere in the universe is the possibility that she will outlast the cancer. Not exactly a strategy you want to have, but if it is your last hope, you hope. So we feed her with stories, and pictures and words. Each day, feeling as though it may be her last, becomes a rally, a celebration. I feel as though I am living years right now with her, because the moments are so beautiful, so exquisite that I will cherish them forever.

To: Ali
From: Kathleen
Date: November 6, 2001
Subj: hi

Got your phone message. I heard it ringing but the kids were rowdy in the bathtub. No chance for diving for a phone when Bongo is partying in the tub. God, am I exhausted. I think God is carrying me right now.

My friend Gini showed up in the parking lot at school today with dinner for my family and I had told her this morning that I didn't need any help. It feels like things are working despite the stress… lots of little things help.

Did I tell you — I'm tired and I don't remember — the other night I asked for a miracle. Five hundred calories a day my mother is getting through the glucose drip. But if we feed her with love and pictures and stories and visitors... while we wait... maybe, just maybe, the cancer will starve.

To: Ali
From: Kathleen
Date: November 10, 2001
Subj: hi

Today it feels like the sea is closing. It parted for two weeks and we all gathered. But now my mom requires so much medication to keep her stable that she has lost her lucidity. She speaks but does not make sense. Desperately, we try to adjust the medicines to make her stable but lucid. The battle is against the raging nausea, the advancing tumor. Maybe this evening she'll be more present. Maybe not. If this goes on for days, she's asked us to take her off fluids. God, how will we do this? How can we not?

To: Ali
From: Kathleen
Date: November 11, 2001
Subj: hi

Yesterday, I watched one of my brothers say goodbye to my mom and today I watched my other brother say goodbye. My sister leaves this afternoon. She'll be back sometime this week. My aunt sleeps at the hospital and my dad and I drive out there again and again. But my mom is going. The medication required to keep her free of nausea increases and she loses her clarity. She sleeps. She can't keep her eyes open. She fights to stay awake. But she goes. So it is.

To: Ali
From: Kathleen
Date: November 11, 2001
Subj: Sunday afternoon

This afternoon I drove back out to the hospital. I'm so tired now. I almost can't focus on the computer screen. I'm not sure if I'm breathing, at least not much. I'm in a fog. Numb. What was I trying to tell you? Oh, I know, I stopped at Borders to buy three CDs before going to the hospital.

At the hospital today, my mom said, "Dad says I'm fighting a war, but I don't like to think of it that way." My mom paused. She was talking to my sister and Joyce, my favorite nurse. "How can I think of it?" she turned to me.

I didn't know what to say, and then something came to me.

"Mom, you are the essence of beauty. You are so refined right now, that there is nothing left but beauty. That is what you are and what you are about." My mother smiled, and my dad's eyes filled with tears. "I like that much better," he said, "It is true."

And then Joyce told my mother what an honor and pleasure it has been knowing her and kissed her on the cheek.

Joyce had a CD player and we put on one of my mom's favorite songs — Rod Stewart's "You're in My Heart, You're in My Soul." My sister and I sat on the couch, listened to the music and watched as my dad held my mom and rocked her gently side to side.

To: Ali
From: Kathleen
Date: November 13, 2001
Subj: hi

I woke pissy today, drove out to the hospital to relieve my dad and see my mom. She was exhausted and wanted to sleep. He'd kept her up visiting.

"Will you let me sleep?" she asked.

"Of course I will mom," I said.

I got her tucked in, the IV lines straight, the tumor drain straight, the stomach drain straight, the pillow in her arms, the one behind her back, the blanket between her knees. I closed the blinds and turned off the ringer on the phone.

"He's difficult, isn't he?" she murmured.

"Dad?" I asked.

"Yes," she said.

"How was he difficult today?" I asked.

"He wanted me to keep talking. He wouldn't let me sleep."

"Sleep," I said. And then I asked, "May I sleep with you?"

"That would be nice," she said.

I curled up beside her, pulled another blanket over myself. I held her in my arms and we slept.

To: Ali
From: Kathleen
Date: November 18, 2001
Subj: hi

I am fried. 24 hours we have someone at the hospital and we take turns in the rotation… and it just seems to go on and on. In a complete delirium, I sorted through our toys today. Control something, right? Now I have a plastic bag full of odd puzzle pieces. I don't even know if we still own some of these puzzles anymore, but I have the pieces all in one bag. Whatever that's worth.

Every article of clothing I own has tissues stuffed in the pockets. When will I get so that I'm not crying that often?

To: Ali
From: Kathleen
Date: November 19, 2001
Subj: hi

It's Monday. Today I head out to the hospital, show up and there is my mother in a wheelchair with the blinds open, lights on having a chat with an old friend of hers who has come from Norway. Hello? I felt like I had seen a ghost, AND my mother is talking about going HOME for Thanksgiving because everyone is coming into town and she doesn't want to miss anything. Hello?

This is a woman who days ago was curled up in a ball retching and moaning for everyone to be quiet and to turn off every light. Even the crack of the light coming through the door's edge was troubling to her.

The doctors and nurses don't know what to say. They all keep coming in and telling my mom the sweetest goodbyes and then they go off duty for a couple of days and when they show up for their rounds, they are so surprised to see that my mom is still alive.

I don't mind taking care of my mother. It's all the driving I'm doing. I live in my car. I drive all day. And then sometimes I get back in my car and head out to the hospital at night. Sunshine needs shoes. She has one pair of flip-flops, and it's getting cold. Bongo's birthday is next week. Not to mention we have Thanksgiving in between. And then there's Sweetness who is understanding when I forget to do things for him. How do I do this motherhood thing?

Today my role was to straighten the catheter cord. I swear to you, I am going crazy. I have so much pent up frustration, anger, sadness, grief, and overwhelm.

To: Lisel
From: Kathleen
Date: November 23, 2001
Subj: hi

It's too late to call. Yesterday was huge. We kidnapped my mom from the hospital and brought her home for seven hours — with her IV pole and everything. It took all three of us to get her in the car — my sister, my dad and me. I held so many lines and bags and machines that buzzed and sounded. We had to pull over three times to get the machine to stop beeping. My mom sat at the head of her dining room table for Thanksgiving dinner. She was unable to eat any food but feasted on all of her family there around her.

Dan's turning off lights and we're off to bed. It feels like a show that's been tremendous and everyone keeps clapping and my mom keeps coming out and doing great encores.

The new plan is that we're bringing my mom home on Monday and getting Hospice to help. We've been rotating 24 hours on duty at the hospital for over a month now. My mom saw that being home was ok so now she's saying she'd like to come home.

To: Lisel
From: Kathleen
Date: November 24, 2001
Subj: hi

I'm collecting the most beautiful, precious memories with my mom. These are moments with my mother, sometimes it's words, but usually it's the lighting coming through the hospital window and how it catches her cheekbones when she smiles. No one would believe it, but without hair, without eyebrows, without eyelashes, my mother is more beautiful. There's nothing at all to distract from the inherent beauty of her face.

I wish I could have all my memories, keep them, treasure them and not have to lose my mom in the exchange.

My heart hurts, but somewhere along the way, I have learned how to love. I continue to be renewed and I continue to find strength, even when it isn't apparent that there's anything in reserve. Such is the beauty of love.

To: Lisel
From: Kathleen
Date: November 25, 2001
Subj: hi

Last night, I took the night shift at the hospital because my
sister is losing it. She's absolutely, totally fried. She's been
dealing with my brothers and my dad for days. In a last-minute
switch, I said I'd stay at the hospital and give my sister a night
off. This was a bigger offer from Dan because Bongo and
Sweetness have both been sick and it meant Dan would most
likely be up in the night with the boys.

Of course, I laughed because it takes going to the hospital for
a "girls' night out" (so much for the giggling trip to Vegas) to
take care of my mother for me to get a good night sleep on a
thin, wavy pull-out couch with metal bars in the mattress.

My mom and I laughed about our slumber party this morning.
Getting up and flipping her over several times in the night
and pushing the call button for a nurse to change her meds
seemed a LUXURY given that at home I have NO call button
and no access to morphine.

I arrive home after an uneventful night at the hospital with
my mom to find Bongo crabby, Dan exhausted, Sunshine
picking fights with Sweetness and Sweetness with a raging
headache — it's probably another sinus infection. I do dishes,
get laundry going, clean up the fort in the playroom, get
toys gathered from the far reaches of the house and make
Sunshine get dressed and clean up her room. Sweetness
gathers Legos from everywhere. I make lunch and feed
everyone. I'm still wearing my clothes from yesterday.

The toilet in Bongo's room is still clogged (three or four days). I
send Dan to my mom's house to get another plunger and I boil

water. I pour boiling water into the toilet and it sends out a vile fume, so vile it sends all of us screaming.

The kids play outside now. Every window in the house is open. Half the house smells like public restrooms in summer at old Phoenix parks. Dan is grumbling about plungers not suctioning. I have not sat down since arriving home, until now.

Should remember… when in need of a moment alone, fill house with putrid scent. It's worth the peace.

To: Ali
From: Kathleen
Date: November 26, 2001
Subj: hi

Today we are bringing my mother home. What this will entail, I don't know. I've left my sister and my dad in charge. I brought in a relief quarterback — my sister. I let her do the scheduling for the last week… and that is not a nice job. 24-hour coverage is difficult. But she did look battle-weary yesterday. Dan and I took her out to dinner to say thank you.

Today is Bongo's birthday. How I am going to pull this off is beyond me. I blew Sweetness's birthday — gifts arrived two weeks late. Grr to myself on that one.

I'm getting a little nerve-wracked about Christmas coming. Tell me that is normal for this time of year. What I am hoping is that with my mom coming home, I'll have a little more time, given that I won't be driving one to two hours a day to the hospital and back.

Dan was trying to convince me to go to San Francisco with him next weekend. I was trying to explain to him, "Honey, moms don't do get-away trips three weeks before Christmas." He didn't get it.

With no party planned in sight for Bongo and very few gifts, I begin today. Last night I was at Albertson's buying him a few presents in the grocery store toy section. Lame. But I was there because I was out of toilet bowl cleaner and laundry detergent. Not to mention olive oil. I honestly can say that I don't believe I have ever run out of laundry detergent. But I am pleased to report that the world doesn't end when one does.

I am joyful my mom is coming home. She's weak, but her clarity is better. She's terribly thin. That's my morning report. Bongo's birthday and my mom coming home.

I found this letter in the purse my mother took
to the hospital the last time she was there.

a letter

Written December 22, 1999

Dear Francie,

I won't go into all of the emotional thoughts that have coursed through my head since Lois called to share the very distressing news of the terrible onslaught to your good health. I probably haven't had a feeling, question, doubt, or concern that you haven't already processed and raised.

What "original" notions I might have to offer in terms of comfort and support are the conclusions I came to when I was beset with cancer myself about 12 years ago. I was diagnosed with a malignant melanoma and after its removal, the only realistic reassurances the doctor could offer me were a set of cold statistics. I turned inside myself to figure out the "what lies ahead" part and how to deal with it, and of course, the thing that kept blurring my thinking were thoughts of my family — in particular, my young daughters.

What I decided that allowed me finally to move on, was that I had spent every minute of every hour of every day loving them very fiercely and with all of my heart and with as much openness and honesty as I could muster. And that this intense devotion had never wavered and that I knew that my family knew that they were the center of my life — and what more could I want and how blessed I was that indeed, I had no regrets behind me and nothing that I would have done differently. Arriving at that state of mind made me very peaceful and gave me the grace to accept whatever the days and years ahead might bring.

And my deep sense of you is that you have also given and loved and shared with your very precious family with such intensity and clarity that your connections are equally rich, viable, and eternal — and that you also have a keen knowledge that you have spent your life exactly as you would have chosen and feel enormously blessed in having had that opportunity.

When you can find the energy to push all that is currently crowding your mind aside and come quietly to this very central part of your being, the overpowering knowledge of your unwavering gift to your family will give you enormous strength to face your illness. And this sense will in turn, give you the peace you need to remove the stress that automatically accompanies such a serious diagnosis and will allow you to focus on your ineffable self — a magnificent woman for all seasons — devoted wife, mother, grandmother, and dear friend.

You are in our prayers and our hearts,
Always and with great affection,

B.J.

To: Ali
From: Kathleen
Date: November 29, 2001
Subj: hi

Things are settling out with my mom being home. I'm getting to
know the new hospice nurses and they are wonderful. People
are visiting and my mom's spirits have never been better. She is
finally well medicated and in no pain and has no nausea.

Today is cold, windy and joyful. Thank God she is home. I can't
even begin to express how wonderful it is for me to walk over to
her house and kiss her cheek. Heaven. I do it many, many times a
day. And it is GREAT for the children because they can run in and
out of her room, say hi and leave and play and come back in and
say something. It feels right and normal to have her home. The
hospital was hard, such a long drive and such hard expectations
on the children. We managed but it was always an ordeal.

But now it all starts to flow again. Home is such a better place
than a hospital. I'm off to clean out rotting food from my fridge.

To: Ali
From: Kathleen
Date: December 01, 2001
Subj: hi

The insanity is cranking up. I have so few days left of kids
in school before Christmas break. It's crazy looking at the
calendar. One day I'm teaching cooking at school and on
another there's a field trip… I think Dan is driving. I went on
a school hike yesterday. It was my sister's last day in town. I
decided to go while she was still here. It was gorgeous being
outside. I held hands with Sweetness and Sunshine 90 percent
of the time. We all needed the time.

To: Lisel
From: Kathleen
Date: December 01, 2001
Subj: hi

Just got your note. Seconds later Dan burst out at me. God, I am living in a tinderbox. He can be such the angry teenager — treating me as if I'm an over-demanding mother. I don't really need another child right now — seeing as I have three and then add my mom.

My mom is home with hospice. Word's out about her impending death — hoards of people come to visit.

Dan was gone on a company retreat for 3 nights. He just returned. He's tired. But so am I. We've been going different directions today taking kids to events. I tell him he's in charge of dinner and he blows. Not that he's unwilling — he's just feeling underappreciated. I did clean the house today, did all his laundry from the retreat, took Sweetness Xmas shopping for his family gifts and 300 other things.

Everything is raw here. We've been at this so long.

I held your note to my heart. God, life is hard sometimes and then the light catches something and it's beautiful.

our holiday letter

December 2001

Dear Friends,

Hello. Today it rains outside. We celebrate this in Arizona because it happens so infrequently. Before the kids had eaten breakfast, they were out playing in it. Sunshine was the first to find the umbrella and spun with it above her head as the rain fell. Bongo put boots on the wrong feet and jumped in the puddles. Sweetness moved houseplants into the rain and then climbed a tree. When it was time to come in, Sweetness closed the umbrella. These are the children: Sunshine is 9, Sweetness is 7 and Bongo is 4.

Our big accomplishment is that after a decade, we are out of diapers. The children eat at restaurants. They sit through movies. They have friends over and sleep until seven. Each small act feels like a miracle. I see these years as golden years. Sunshine still holds my hand while we shop. Sweetness delights in sneaking around the corner and surprising me. And Bongo hugs me in the morning, as if it's been forever since we've seen each other.

Dan's work continues to go well. They moved offices and have a new name. He now has air conditioning, an elevator, and his own office. The biggest perk for me was that they hired a VP of sales in September and so Dan has been home more.

My work has been fun. I have many unfinished projects that I am eager to spend more time on. But mostly, this past year, I have focused on savoring my mother. She has been living with a serious illness and her condition has been unresponsive to various treatments. Now she is home with hospice care and will die soon. As profoundly sad as I am at the prospect of losing her, I am overwhelmed by the fineness of her spirit. She has shown us all how to live and what is worth fighting for, again and again and again.

In Arizona, it is good and right to dance when it rains. My mother knows this. "Isn't the rain wonderful?" she said to me this morning, "Open the door." I did, and the scent of rain filled her room. Together our spirits danced in it. When life looks short, it is ever so dear.

I send my blessings and our love,

Kathleen, Dan, Sunshine, Sweetness and Bongo

To: Ali
From: Kathleen
Date: December 6, 2001
Subj: hi

I can't sleep. I have a splitting headache and I woke crying. It's
so hard this time because there's no place for her to bounce
back from. She's so thin. So very, very thin. Her body's
shutting down. She's going to die. And I felt it for the first time
the day before yesterday. The kids were there singing her silly
Christmas songs and she was with us and then I felt her feel
so tired, so very, very tired. And I felt her start to let go. It is
what is appropriate right now, what is right. But it's hard.

To: Lisel
From: Kathleen
Date: December 7, 2001
Subj: hi

We're trying to determine when to take my mom off fluids.
We were prepared to do it today. Then, in a rare moment of
lucidity, I asked my mom if she was ready and she said, "Not
yet. One or two more days." I called my dad and we're waiting.

I am tired. I just crawl in bed with my mom and hold her. There
is nothing else I can do. And it does seem to help.

Will I make it? Simple to rearrange those words. I will make it.
Difficult to do.

To: Lisel
From: Kathleen
Date: December 10, 2001
Subj: hi

Monday morning here. We took the kids to the ranch on Saturday. Sunshine said she needed it. She said we needed it. So I did it. Packed us all up and we went for one night.

It was hard to leave. We stayed in the new house. A caretaker used to live there and my parents redid it. Every piece of furniture and fabric there my mom chose while she was sick. I saw her fight to keep living, to keep doing.

I cried and then went tobogganing in the snow. We had a snowball fight, built a snowman and then cut our own Christmas tree. A first.

My mom will go soon. It's ok.

To: Lisel
From: Kathleen
Date: December 10, 2001
Subj: you can appreciate this

Today we took my mother off fluids. There was the meeting in the kitchen. Her doctor, my aunt, my father and I were there. Then the doctor met with the hospice nurse. During that time, my dad went into my mother's room and put on the music from "South Pacific." The overture played and the first few songs began. Time passed, the music played. I went into my mother's room and was rubbing her legs. My aunt came in and Maria (my mother's housekeeper and friend for the last twenty years) came in. Maria put lotion on my mom's arms. And Mary Lou had her hands on my mother's back. I was singing to the songs. Then my mother's favorite came on, "Some Enchanted Evening." My father sang this to my mother during their courtship. She says she married him because he can sing. We listened, and then it was hard to listen because the hospice nurse was there in the room fiddling with the machines. She was on the phone, reciting something out loud, too loud. Couldn't she wait? She was following protocol, on the phone with her supervisor, calling out times, 11:47 AM, and fluid amounts and dates, December 10th and doctor's orders. And then as the song ended, the nurse was quiet. I looked at the IV pole. There a loose tube dangled. Something I've never seen on an IV pole. The tubes are always attached. Suddenly, I realized what had happened while "Some Enchanted Evening" played. My mother was taken off fluids. Outside a cold wind blew away dark clouds that had blocked the morning sun. Leaves on the sycamore tree began to fall and turned golden in the late morning light. The air was filled with gold and the moment was perfect.

Part IV

white cyclamen

a card

Written in December of 2001

Dear Kathleen,

It was sad to learn of your dear mother's passing. I think of her often as I listen to my sons practice their piano. I think all the memories of watching you practice the piano during our play dates really inspired me to have my sons study piano. (I always wished I could play like you.)

Simply kind is how I remember her. She always made me feel welcome.

I am sorry for your pain and loss but joyful for the life she now knows free of pain and tears. I know God will continue to bless your family.

Thank you for all the happy memories of days gone by.

Love,

Catherine

a letter

December 17, 2001

Dear Kathleen,

When I read your mother's obituary in the paper, I knew that at last her suffering had ended but I worried about you, Kathleen, and your siblings and of course, your father and all the grandchildren.

I hope that the examples she set for you will help you through this very difficult time. She was a beautiful lady, much admired and respected, and she would want you to carry on in your lives. It will always be different for you living without her but you are only without her in the physical sense because she lives on in hundreds of ways. You will keep her spirit alive in your heart. The children which you and Dan brought into this world and which she loved so dearly will remember her not only from first-hand experiences, but also from the details you supply them with stories from your childhood, your memories of the love you felt in receiving a rich and beautiful love from her.

You are young to have lost your mother. She was young to have died. Some years back I remember reading the articles you wrote, which were published in the local paper. Maybe later, after the bitter pain has subsided, you can resume your writing. You do have that gift, that talent for putting words on paper which affect people in a good way. I remember that your words made me laugh. You probably are far away from being able to do that but maybe in time....

Know that I am thinking of you and Dan.

Love,

Elizabeth

To: Ali
From: Kathleen
Date: December 17, 2001
Subj: hi

Just picked up my mom's ashes with my dad and brought her
home. Went to the grocery store before that, made chili, will
rest for 10 minutes and then pick kids up at school and take
them to swim practice. Isn't this strange? It feels strange. Very
surreal. All these people hugging me, crying. Maybe I'm numb
today. Will send you a copy of the obit. I think I'm in shock.

To: Ali
From: Kathleen
Date: December 17, 2001
Subj: hi

I read to my boys tonight. Three books and it felt good to
hold them and to read. To not be racing over to my mom's,
throwing kids and homework at Dan. To not be reading and
torn that I wasn't at my mom's. To not be at my mom's sorry to
be missing my kids. What a crazy, crazy time this had been. I
woke so relieved today to not have to be dealing with doctors
and nurses and meds, to not have to see my mom suffering.
To not have to fight to get more pain meds ordered. To not
have to watch her dry-heaving. Such relief and such sadness.

My dad just arrived. I have chili for him, he loves it. Must go.

To: Lisel
From: Kathleen
Date: February 19, 2002
Subj: hi

Two sick boys home from school today. One minute they're flopped on the couch and the next they're begging to go on a bike ride. I compromised and took them to the neighbor's to pick tangerines.

Now Sweetness plays piano. Bongo's in the tub. Sunshine's working at the computer. When a child practices piano, everything feels right in the world. I cook. They play piano. Heaven.

After Dan got home, I went to my mom's house. I haven't been there in weeks. I was alone there. It was OK. I found an old photo album. It felt like I was guided to it — I hadn't seen it in decades. Inside there was a photograph of my grandmother, Mama Forest, my mom and me — just taken, not posed. It felt comforting to see all of us together. I walked home feeling the separateness that hurts these days is more illusion — and the connection in the photo, more truth.

Bedtime calls.

our holiday letter
December 2002

Dear Friends,

Hello. Fortunately, our biggest news this year is that our sweet Lily got married. It was a shotgun wedding, but few seemed to hold it against her. The only disgruntled party member was the chauffeur. As I was away, Dan assumed all responsibility for the weekend (payback for a guys' fishing trip). And so Dan, God bless him, passed the better part of a Saturday escorting 10-year-old girls to wedding events. Two weeks later, Lily blessed us with the arrival of five dwarf hamsters and any impropriety associated with their birth was forgotten.

As for other news, Bongo, age 5, has asked that we call him Harry Potter. Most often he wears a cape, travels by broom and waves a wand. He fights great battles and emerges victorious after glory and hardship. He keeps us laughing. Recently, I told him his voice sounded hoarse. He gave me a deep, raspy reply, "Mama, my voice is changing, that happens when boys grow up."

Sweetness, age 8, has taken an interest in reading the morning paper. This creates difficult questions before 7 am. He plays the piano with elbows out and fingers flying. He has become our in-house, fix-it man and likes electronics, particularly alarm clocks. One night, he and Sunshine set several alarms in our room to ensure we were all awake for a meteor shower. Not only did I see the meteors, I saw the sun rise.

Sunshine, age 10, recently won her student council election on the platform that she loves to plan parties. After the hamster wedding, Sunshine convinced Sweetness to invite all of her friends to his birthday party so the girls could run a haunted house for the boys. Sunshine made to-do lists for every family member, and I spent a week checking off my items. With eyeballs, guts and brains, the party was a huge success and several parents offered to hire her.

Dan is doing well. He has a great team at work and they're excited about what they're doing. At home, he finally turned over the responsibility of mowing the lawn to a gardener. With more time, Dan has taken it upon himself to see that our dog Rosie gets in shape. "Eat less and exercise more," is his motto and we're pleased to report it is working quite well for the dog.

My news is that I have time for flowers again. I potted cyclamen. These floppy white flowers look like angels dancing, particularly when they've been watered. My goal is to water them before they fall over. Seems much of life is similar. My other news is that I am writing again. I unplug the phone and write. I'm loving it.

I want to mention that I was unable to respond to many of the condolence cards sent to me. Please know, I was profoundly touched by your words and prayers of support. Thank you for being there for me.

Wishing you blessings and bits of wonder.

Kathleen, Dan, Sunshine, Sweetness, Bongo, Rosie, Lily and Spot (one of Lily's daughter's)

Written 1996
Published Sunday, March 2, 1997
The Los Angeles Times

Post-Its and Motherhood

Before the invention of yellow Post-its, my mother wore rubber bands on her wrists to remind her of what it was she had to do. Often her fingers turned blue from the lack of circulation. But my mother is a practical woman, and she would use the tingling sensation in her fingers to draw attention to the rubber bands and the tasks they symbolized.

Many memories I have are of my mother stopping everything she was doing to touch one of the colored rubber bands on her wrist. Out loud, she would wonder what it was that she had to remember.

"The green one was to remind me to take the chicken out of the oven," she'd say. "The yellow one was to remind me to send book money to school with two of you." She'd be lost in thought. "The brown ones are all household items, nothing critical. But the red one, what was the red one for?"

We'd all hold still, aware of the seriousness of the moment, and speak only to offer suggestions.

"Candy," my sister would call out.

"More clothes for me," I would suggest.

"No, no," my mother would say, distracted by trying to recall the forgotten item. Then the stress would break with her recollection. "Oh, yes. I need to pick up your brothers at the mall."

The advent of Post-its improved my mother's life as well as her hand circulation. But initially, she had to overcome the problem of not being able to wear the yellow squares of paper. Always quick to find solutions, she set about transforming the appearance of our home.

Her bathroom mirror, a place where I loved to admire myself as I tried on her makeup and jewelry, became a mosaic of yellow sticky paper. The Post-its in the bathroom always seemed to involve self-improvement or family betterment. "Do exercises." "Laugh more." "Discuss vocabulary words at dinner." My mother, true to her lists, would work on these items every day. But in the mornings, I would watch her hunched over, searching for a vacant space at the lower edge of the mirror for a reflection from which she could apply her lipstick.

Our kitchen changed as well. The hood that hung over our stovetop turned into a fire hazard. My mother developed an elaborate system of Post-it attached to Post-it, eight or nine squares deep, all dangling in a row from the stainless steel surface. Each column represented a child's needs and was arranged in birth order. Additional columns were for grocery store lists and social correspondences. When several pots on the stove were boiling at the same time, the hot air would make the columns of yellow sticky paper dance like silent wind chimes caught in a gale.

Before Post-its, my mother stored extra rubber bands in her car on the gearshift. As she drove, she would recall things she needed to remember and would slide onto her wrist more and more rubber bands. But after Post-its, the rubber bands were discarded and the steering wheel transformed from a circle into a pinwheel that spun around with yellow flags waving.

It's no wonder my mother always seemed to be omnipresent. If she wasn't around, her lists were.

Of course, our refrigerator changed too. On top of the holiday photographs and school memos was plastered a series of messages. My mother's handwriting defies gravity, form or consistency. She insists she was supposed to be left-handed, but nuns forced her to use her right hand for writing. One afternoon, I was trying to decode some of my mother's notes on the refrigerator. I deciphered a few, "Buy milk." "Call Bank." "Turn off garden hose." And then I saw one I couldn't understand. "Grandpa George's ashes. Where are they???" Grandpa George was my mother's father.

I confronted my mother with the note. "Is this really what this says?"

She assured me not to worry, that there was some note stuck on some prominent place around the house to remind her of where she had put Grandpa George. I pointed out that the kitchen faucet, the headboard on her bed, even the wall space in every bathroom just above the toilet paper rolls were covered in Post-its. But she didn't seem worried.

"He'll show up," she said. "Besides, he'd think it was funny," she said and laughed.

I didn't inherit the same sense of humor. On that day, I vowed I'd never be a list-maker. But all of this occurred before I had children.

As a child and then later as an adult with no children, I was certain my mother was born a list-maker. I never once thought that perhaps we had driven her to such extreme behavior, that maybe her lists had less to do with her and more to do with us.

And now I know.

Mothers don't choose to be list-makers. Either it happens or you lose your mind. Initially, after the birth of my first child, I thought I could survive on mental lists alone. As I prepared to leave home, I would chant to myself, "Wipes, car keys and snacks. Wipes, car keys and snacks."

I soon found that the number of times I had been awakened during the night reduced the number of items I could remember. I gave up and purchased blue Post-its. I thought the color would assure I would be different than my mother.

At first, I made lists cautiously, terribly aware of where an obsession could lead, but I quickly saw there were too many things I had to remember to take with me, to buy, to do and not to do. I didn't know that agreeing to care for a baby also meant caring for a home. The combination of responsibilities guaranteed I would convert to a lifestyle of list-making.

On reflection, I am certain that if I could gather all the lists my mother made over the years, the total would inspire awe. Compiled in her nearly illegible handwriting, these notes would tell a story of simple needs and daily goals, a life dedicated to caring for people.

The big accomplishments in life make headlines or money, but what I have come to realize and appreciate is that life is not held together by fame and fortune. Life is held together by Post-its and mothers.

dear reader

I imagine our teacups are empty, but it is my hope that our hearts are full. At first I was sorry this story was mine. I didn't want it to be my mom who had gotten sick. It isn't the story I would have written, but it is the story I lived. The hardest part was looking at it. When I did, I saw why the pain was there. There was so much pain, because there was so much love.

People have asked me how I was able to put this story together. I had support from dear friends. I took e-mails and letters to their kitchens and read them out loud. Sometimes teenagers passed through, asking for money or food. Other times grandchildren toddled about eating Cheerios from plastic cups. As mothers, grandmothers, daughters, we cried together, drank tea and ate chocolate. We also laughed — remembering times passed.

After rereading all of these e-mails, letters and columns, I feel grateful. I am grateful for this story and that it is mine. I also feel grateful for love. No one, nothing, not even death, can take that away. Love is. And it still is.

There you have it — that's the story I found in the Tiffany box.

xxoo Kathleen

I loved flying. I mean I really loved flying.
I flew a two-seater, a Piper Cub. I'd top off the gas tank,
and then I'd take off and stay up for as long as I could.
I'd watch my gas gauge and I'd keep flying.
I'd fly and fly and fly, and then
I'd bring her in on empty.

Francie Mallery

about the author

Photo: Brad Reed

Kathleen Buckstaff lives with her husband and their three children in the San Francisco Bay area. In addition to writing columns, plays and books, Kathleen works as a performance artist. With the help of Artistic Director Carol MacLeod, Kathleen wrote a one-woman play using the e-mails, letters, columns and diary entries contained in this story.

"The Tiffany Box, a love remembered" opened at the Theatre Artist Studio in Phoenix, AZ on November 4, 2010. Kathleen performed the play to sold-out theatres in Phoenix and San Francisco. She performed the play again in New York City as part of a solo festival, and "*The Tiffany Box*" was selected as one of the most outstanding plays.

Kathleen received a BA in English and Creative Writing from Stanford and a MA in Journalism from Stanford.

The author extends her gratitude and love to her husband and children.

For more stories and Book Club discussion questions, please visit: kathleenbuckstaff.com.